Harvard historical monographs.

ALTERATIONS OF

THE WORDS OF JESUS

AS QUOTED IN THE LITERATURE

OF THE SECOND CENTURY

LEON E. WRIGHT

Associate Professor of New Testament

Howard University

HARVARD UNIVERSITY PRESS

Cambridge, Massachusetts

1952

PRINTED IN THE UNITED STATES OF AMERICA

To the Memory of My Grandmother

Preface

The motivated alterations of the words of Jesus have been, it is hoped, objectively examined here in relation to the "life situation" of the early Christian community. One cannot overestimate the value of proper perspective in this area for the formulation of correct historical judgments on the sociological, as well as theological, experiences of the primitive church.

I have desired to make available the investigation of sources to as large a circle of historical scholarship as possible. To this end, Greek words in quotations used in the body of this monograph have been translated. The Revised Standard Version of the New Testament has been the source for the translation of the control models which appear in this work. As for patristic and other citations, although I have occasionally taken slight liberties with certain renderings here, these translations present no significant variation from such standard sources as the *Ante-Nicene Fathers*, the Loeb Classical Library, or M. R. James's *Apocryphal New Testament*.

This study had its inception as a Ph.D. dissertation submitted to the Department of the History and Philosophy of Religion at Harvard University, April 1945. Then, as more recently, Professor Henry J. Cadbury, through invaluable suggestions and criticisms, contributed importantly to the form and substance of this research. He is aware, I feel, of the gratitude which I cannot adequately express. To the Administration of Howard University, Dr. Richard W. Hale, Jr., Mr. David K. Niles, and Mrs. Jennie Grossinger, I am deeply appreciative for indispensable encouragement and assistance toward the completion of this effort. Finally, I should like to thank Professor William H. P. Hatch, another of my teachers, who has graciously lent his scholarly resources to the tedious task of proofreading these pages.

L. E. W.

Cambridge, Massachusetts
September 1950

Contents

APPENDICES

PART ONE

Patristic Quotation

TU: Texte und Untersuchungen zur altchristlichen Literatur

ZNW: Zeitschrift für die neutestamentliche Wissenschaft

I

Introduction

The fact of variant readings in the transmission of the text of the New Testament is too abundantly evident for either refutation or defense. Nor again are their causes difficult to discern. Indeed, "In the beginning there were not two ways of copying the New Testament — as there were with the classics — the more correct way, with expert copyists as workmen, and the less careful way, with amateur scribes at work. In fact, it would seem that during the first three centuries the second way was the only one known." [1] It is very probable, also, that during the course of these early centuries local scribes and private individuals engaged in uncontrolled copying of the books of the New Testament with a frequency and freedom more usual than exceptional.[2] Such unsystematic, provincial reproduction of the New Testament text, and that by men given more to consideration for content than to regard for form, led inevitably to the complex diversity of readings which no critical apparatus perhaps even now adequately records.

That very many, or even most, of these variants had their genesis in errors arising out of the physical or educational

[1] Leo Vaganay, *An Introduction to the Textual Criticism of the New Testament*, trans. B. V. Miller (St. Louis, Mo., 1937), pp. 75f.

[2] F. G. Kenyon, *Recent Developments in the Textual Criticism of the Greek Bible* (London, 1939), p. 76.

limitations of the copyist, and so were of an unconscious or unintentional order, seems patent. And although errors of memory, eye, pen, or speech may not be quite so neatly isolated as certain nomenclatures would suggest, such imperfections are necessary concomitants, in varying degrees, of the process of transcription on whatever level.[3]

In further accounting for textual variation resultant upon such decentralized transmission, Kenyon observes: "In these circumstances we have to envisage the growth, in the second and third centuries, of a large number of local texts. . . As the papyrus codex came into use (which may now be ascribed to the third century, and perhaps even to the second), and as at the same time the demand grew for a precise delimitation of the authoritative books of the faith, we must imagine a process of collection of rolls from various sources, of the transcription of the several Gospels into a single codex, and of the commencement of a critical comparison of texts. . . It would be just as likely to take the form of incorporating new incidents or new phrases wherever they were found, or of assimilating the narrative in one Gospel to that in another, as of seeking austerely to preserve an uncontaminated tradition."[4]

If Kenyon is correct in his reconstruction, it is just this conscious process of interpolation, assimilation, selection by scribe or editor which poses the most serious consideration under the heading of textual variation. It is to this problem that we shall address ourselves, in a specific connection, in the development of this monograph. Yet, though the phe-

---

[3] For a succinct discussion of the several categories to which many textual changes may be assigned, see Nestle's *Einführung in das Neue Testament*, umgearbeitet von E. von Dobschütz (Göttingen, 1923), pp. 2–7; A. T. Robertson's *Introduction to the Textual Criticism of the New Testament* (New York, 1925), pp. 150–160; and R. P. Lagrange's "Projet de critique textuelle rationelle du Nouveau Testament," *Revue Biblique*, XLII (1933), 496.

[4] Kenyon, p. 77.

nomenon of "nonaccidental" variation be accepted as proved, discussion still proceeds concerning the degree to which this liberty has been indulged. Does the range extend clearly from a meticulous attendance upon small detail to personal or sectarian considerations of doctrinal preference?

Much modern debate on this question has had its point of departure in certain statements of Dr. Hort's which are classically set forth in his Introduction. Dr. Hort asserts:

"It will not be out of place to add here a distinct expression of our belief that even among the numerous unquestionably spurious readings of the New Testament there are no signs of deliberate falsification of the text for dogmatic purposes. The licence of paraphrase occasionally assumes the appearance of wilful corruption, where scribes allowed themselves to change language which they thought capable of dangerous misconstruction; or attempted to correct apparent errors which they doubtless assumed to be due to previous transcription; or embodied in explicit words a meaning which they supposed to be implied. . . In a word, they bear witness to rashness, not to bad faith.

"It is true that dogmatic preferences to a great extent determined theologians, and probably scribes, in their choice between rival readings already in existence. . . Accusations of wilful tampering with the text are accordingly not unfrequent in Christian antiquity: but, with a single exception, wherever they can be verified they prove to be groundless, being in fact hasty and unjust inferences from mere diversities of inherited text. The one known exception is in the case of Marcion's dogmatic mutilation of the books accepted by him: and this was, strictly speaking, an adaptation for the use of his followers." [5]

It appears from this assertion that Dr. Hort is at pains to validate the essential purity of canonical tradition and the

[5] B. F. Westcott and F. J. A. Hort, *The New Testament in the Original Greek* (2 vols.; Cambridge and London, 1882), II, Introduction, 282f.

trustworthiness of its transmission so far as this tradition has been recovered and selected according to approved textual norms.[6] There is, too, the seemingly corroborative opinion of Kirsopp Lake wherein he states, "It is probable, though not certain, that dogmatic reasons may have caused alterations."[7] Lake likewise adduces Marcion as the single "known" exception.

In opposition to Dr. Hort's thesis, however, are pronouncements by such critics as Rendel Harris[8] and W. F. Howard,[9] to mention but these two. On the other hand, their relatively few genuine findings by way of rebuttal, coupled with Lake's cautious opinion, appear to constitute a strong presumption for at least the basic acceptance of Dr. Hort's optimism. Yet Lake himself elsewhere[10] demonstrates quite convincingly (though on other than textual or documentary grounds, which are here inconclusive) the ineptness and the "primitive" improbability of baptismal conditions and injunctions in the text of our Gospels, especially as found in Matthew xxviii.19 and John iii.5. From this paucity of direct evidence Lake nevertheless concludes that such a situation "shows

[6] Dr. Hort declares further (p. 284), "The books of the New Testament as preserved in extant documents [and in Codex B in particular] assuredly speak to us in every important respect in language identical with that in which they spoke to those for whom they were originally written." But, since B is here regarded as the touchstone of this transmissional purity, it should be noted that more recent criticism dissents in the ascription of such unique excellence to the Vatican manuscript. Cf. Kenyon, p. 82; B. H. Streeter, *The Four Gospels* (London, 1930), pp. 6of.; Kirsopp Lake, *The Text of the New Testament*, revised by Silva New (6th ed.; London, 1949), p. 86.

[7] Lake, p. 6.

[8] See his *Sidelights on New Testament Research* (London, 1908), Lecture I and Appendix; "New Points of View in Textual Criticism," *The Expositor*, VII (1914), 316–334.

[9] "The Influence of Doctrine upon the Text of the New Testament," *London Quarterly and Holborn Review*, X (1941), 1–16.

[10] "The Influence of Textual Criticism on the Exegesis of the New Testament": An Inaugural Lecture Delivered before the University of Leiden, January 27, 1904.

that in doctrinal modifications of the text, which are almost
sure to be very early [earlier, in fact, than our actual manu-
scripts], it is vain to ask for much manuscript evidence." [11]
And again, "The fact that so few variants can certainly be
traced to this cause is probably due to the vigilance with
which the orthodox and the heretics regarded each other's
efforts in this direction." [12] Thus Lake is seen merely to issue
a note of restraint in reference to a textual situation of which
not too much can be urged in the nature of its limitations.

To be sure, the balance of probability seems reasonably to
point to the fact of change (however slight) in the text of
the New Testament deriving no less frequently from dogmatic than from other motivation. Although traces of this
activity are very likely obscured by the kind of reciprocal
diligence which Lake suggests, the probability nevertheless

---

[11] *Ibid.*, p. 10. Maurice Goguel writes in similar vein in his *Le Texte et
les éditions du Nouveau Testament grec* (Paris, 1920), p. 67.

[12] *Text of the New Testament*, p. 6. A merely suggestive summary of
some instances of textual variation in our Gospels traceable to dogmatic
motivation may be here properly listed. In addition to Professor Lake's
investigation, Rendel Harris, W. F. Howard, and Maurice Goguel mention
and discuss, among others, the following occurrences. In Jn. vii.8 οὔπω is
inserted for οὐκ ἀναβαίνω in MSS B L Δ Λ. Instead of αὐτούς, πάντας is added
to ἐθεράπευσεν in D a b c g Syr[s] with reference to Mt. iv.24. In Mt. i.16 the
Sinaitic Syriac reads: Ἰωσὴφ δὲ ᾧ ἐμνηστεύθη Μαριὰμ ἡ παοθένος ἐγέννησεν
Ἰησοῦν χριστόν; most of the Old Latin, a g k q Syr[c] Arm and four minuscules
read: Ἰωσήφ, ᾧ μνηστευθεῖσα ἡ παρθένος Μαρία ἐγέννησεν τὸν Ἰησοῦν χριστόν
(q omits *virgo*); as over against the reading found in all our Greek uncials,
and almost all the minuscules: Ἰωσὴφ τὸν ἄνδρα Μαρίας ἐξ ἧς ἐγεννήθη Ἰησοῦς
ὁ λεγόμενος Χριστός. In Lk. ii.43, Mary and Joseph are called the parents of
Jesus (οἱ γονεῖς αὐτοῦ), but the substitution Ἰωσὴφ καὶ ἡ μήτηρ αὐτοῦ obtains
in A C N X. MS 76 reads τοῦ καθαρισμοῦ αὐτῆς, a substitution for αὐτῶν
in Lk. ii.22. There is also the omission of the "bloody sweat" and of the
sustaining angel in Lk. xxii.43–44 by אᵃ B N Syrˢ. The substitution of θεός
for υἱός with μονογενής in Jn. i.18 is found in א B C*. Further, D, with other
Western support, omits the statement of Jesus' rearing in Nazareth, also
the word αὐτῷ in connection with εἰωθός in Lk. iv.16. "The Elect of God" is
read instead of "Son of God" in two cursives, Syrᶜ˒ˢ א* a b P⁵ in connection
with Jn. i.34. The prayer for forgiveness is omitted from Lk. xxiii.34 by
B D* W Θ אᵃ Syrˢ.

exists quite apart from our present inability readily to identify the signs. Certainly such textual changes are significant
historically in so far as they stem each from some definite
religious experience or conviction on the part of the early
church. To such an extent, textual criticism becomes more
than a mere "algebra of combinations." Rather, it imposes
strongly its claim to be heard as a "historical discipline" sup-
plementing with authority our reconstruction of ecclesiastical
history on other grounds.[13]

To what extent, then, is the phenomenon of conscious textual adaptation operative and discernible in the corpus of
patristic [14] quotations recoverable in the literature of the
second century? More specifically, what is the degree of accuracy achieved in this body of evidence so far as sayings of
Jesus are purportedly set forth? And in the event of proved
deviation with intent from canonical norms,[15] what does such
discrepancy argue as to motive?

The presumption that with increasing authoritative definition of the canon of the New Testament there arose a corresponding reverence for the *ipsissima verba* of the now sacred
corpus, at least with reference to patristic treatment of this
text, will be seen to require some revision. This problem has

[13] See D. W. Riddle, "Textual Criticism as a Historical Discipline,"
Anglican Theological Review, XVIII (1936), 220–233. Note also Howard's
quotations of C. H. Turner and Rendel Harris on p. 6 of his article in the
London Quarterly and Holborn Review, referred to above.

[14] The term "patristic" is here enlarged to include all dominical quotations,
orthodox and heterodox, which may reasonably be assigned to the second
century.

[15] The biblical text of Westcott and Hort has been made the working
basis of this investigation. Such use is not intended to imply for this so-
called "Neutral" text, however, the unique textual superiority claimed for it
by Drs. Westcott and Hort. For contemporary textual critics, the Greek text
of final authority, in the light of available evidence, is an eclectic one.
Nevertheless, "the Westcott-Hort text is still the great classical edition of
modern times" (F. C. Grant, "The Greek Text of the New Testament," *An
Introduction to the Revised Standard Version of the New Testament*, p. 41).

been previously dealt with within the limits of the writings of Justin Martyr and Clement of Alexandria.[16] It is at once obvious, however, that both Justin Martyr and Clement of Alexandria occupy a more or less "transitional" position, since the rigid idea of canonicity had not yet become fixed in either Roman or Alexandrian tradition. Justin is still able to supplement the gospel sayings with oral tradition; [17] nor is he above elaborating the gospel story by means of apocryphal details.[18] For Clement of Alexandria, Barnabas is "the apostle." [19] The epistle of Clement of Rome is "Scripture." [20] And the Shepherd of Hermas speaks even now with compelling inspiration ($\theta\epsilon\dot{\iota}\omega\varsigma$).[21] Hence, in order that a substantial appraisal may be made of the standard of accuracy of quotation within the pale of canonical tradition, it seems imperative that we go beyond these limits. Irenaeus and Tertullian have thus been included in this survey as representative of a period of relatively mature canonical development. And the limits of the second century have been transcended for a supplementary consideration of the quotations of Origen (Appendix D), a writer of prodigiously wide and fruitful interests in strictly textual, as well as theological, affairs. It has been generally believed that we may assume a standard for Origen which we cannot claim for others. However sound this may be, even in Origen, the molding dynamics of motivating interests of a religious and practical character will be seen clearly to have come to expression.

[16] E. L. Titus submitted at the University of Chicago, June 1942, a doctoral thesis entitled "The Motivation of Changes Made in the New Testament Text by Justin Martyr and Clement of Alexandria."

[17] *Dial.* 35.47.

[18] *Dial.* 69.78.

[19] *Strom.* ii.6.

[20] *Strom.* iv.17.

[21] *Strom.* ii.12.

B. THE WORDS OF JESUS

In treating of patristic quotation of the sayings of Jesus, we appear to run afoul of two mutually exclusive considerations. The first is the demonstrably lax method of quotation in antiquity. The second is the high priority accorded the words of Jesus in the Christian community. An exclusive consideration of either factor would predispose us to misjudgment of the other. Both phenomena must be touched upon for proper historical perspective in our discussion.

It is more or less consistently to be observed that, in early ecclesiastical writings, longer quotations are usually made with an appreciably higher degree of accuracy than are the shorter excerpts. Dr. Sanday, after an examination of some ninety Old Testament quotations made by Clement of Rome, observes the trend of accuracy to be strongly in favor of the longer passages. He finds, in fact, only "two passages of more than three consecutive verses in length that present wide divergences." He concludes: "This is perhaps what we should expect: in longer quotations it would be better worth the writer's while to refer to his cumbrous manuscript. These purely mechanical conditions are too much lost sight of. We must remember that the ancient writer had not a small compact reference Bible at his side, but, when he wished to verify a reference, would have to take an unwieldy roll out of its case, and then would not find it divided into chapter and verse like our modern books, but would have only the columns, and those, perhaps not numbered, to guide him. We must remember too that the memory was much more practised and relied upon in ancient times, especially among the Jews." [22]

Even if it can be shown, as Kenyon believes probable on

[22] W. Sanday, *The Gospels in the Second Century* (London, 1876), pp. 29f. May not these findings indicate, too, a "difference in habit" of quotation by some Fathers in their use of the Old Testament as compared with their treatment of the more familiar New Testament?

the basis of the Chester Beatty Papyri, that the use of the biblical codex may be assigned to the second century, the page still lacked adequate symbols to facilitate reference. The resort to memory, wherever possible, would thus necessarily become the normal procedure. Hence, use of the biblical text under these circumstances, making for assimilation to and combination of parallel passages of Scripture or for allusive or paraphrastic rendering, furnishes little as to motive or even as to source. The fact of indirect quotation, although relatively infrequent, and that of quotation without acknowledgment also deserve mention in any assessment of patristic method. These phenomena seem, further, to impose certain limits upon the critic, so that, for example, it cannot be urged from his silence that Justin did not know by name our canonical Gospels; [23] nor is the judgment above question which postulates a gospel harmony as his source solely on the strength of his by no means consistent combination of parallel material. (To be sure, as Professor Lake cautions,[24] the matter of quotation from some gospel harmony must

[23] "At the outset it is well for us to consider what we may justly look for in the books of this time that will be of use to us in proving the existence and defining the authoritative character of the writings of the New Testament. To put the extreme case, some critics seem to look for . . . a completeness of reference as the only due and acceptable testimony to the presence and valuation of the New Testament. . . Others are apparently surprised to find that any author fails to name or at least quote most accurately every solitary book in the New Testament, and they find the lack of both for any book a sure sign that the missing book was not then in existence or not then known to the writer. So far from that does the everyday literary habit diverge, that we must on the contrary be profoundly grateful when an early writer mentions any one of the books by name, and find great satisfaction and security even if he does not mention the name, if he offer us sentences which, even if rewrought with editorial licence, clearly point to the said book as their source. We should never forget that these writers did not write for the purpose of giving us proofs of the authority of the New Testament books" (C. R. Gregory, *Canon and Text of the New Testament*, New York, 1907, pp. 6of.).

[24] *Text of the New Testament*, p. 50.

never be excluded as a real possibility in one's dealing with
patristic treatment of evangelic sources.)

We are at once confronted with an egregious paradox, however, as we attempt to apply method to material. For we
have here to do with the words of Jesus, from the very outset to be "remembered" [25] in the Christian community with
the authority of divine law. Origen, in fact, expressed a fundamental judgment of the early church with the declaration
that, though they were "wise" and worthy of all belief
(εὔπιστα), the apostolic writings were decidedly inferior to
the words of the Lord (οὐ μὴν παραπλήσια τῷ Τάδε λέγει
κύριος παντοκράτωρ).[26] Indeed, by this time, the Gospels
had become the "first fruit of all Scripture." Harnack devel-
ops the matter historically thus: "The earliest motive force,
one that had been at work from the beginning of the Apostolic
Age, was the supreme reverence in which the words and
teaching of Christ Jesus were held. I have purposely used
the expression 'supreme reverence,' for in the ideas of those
days inspiration and authority had their degrees. Not only
were the spirits of the prophets subject to the prophets, but
there were recognised degrees of higher and highest in their
utterances. . . He Himself had often introduced His message with the words 'I am come' (*i.e.* to do something which
had not yet been done), or, 'But I say unto you' (in opposition to something that had been hitherto said). This claim
received its complete recognition among the disciples in the
unswerving conviction that the words and directions of
Jesus formed the supreme rule of life. Thus side by side with
the writings of the Old Testament appeared the Word of
'the Lord,' and not only so, but in the formula αἱ γραφαὶ καὶ
ὁ Κύριος the two terms were not only of equal authority, but
the second unwritten term received a stronger accent than

[25] Acts xx.35.
[26] Origen, *Comm. in Joan.* i.3.

the first that had literary form." [27] And although the anti-Montanist (writing, as Harnack thinks, about 192–193) [28] expressed his reverence and precaution in terms convenient to his polemic, he also reflected a response basic to the piety of the Christian church from the very outset with reference to the things which Jesus began to preach and to say.

Again, therefore, we may inquire: With what liberty has this sacred deposit been drawn upon? What is the nature and temper of the ideas for which the authority of dominical pronouncement ($\lambda\acute{\epsilon}\gamma\epsilon\iota$ $'I\eta\sigma\circ\hat{v}\varsigma$) has been enlisted? Thus our interest in the textual deviations of second-century literature will be limited in no sense to an academic preoccupation for accuracy of quotation. We are to observe also in these divergences, whether original with a given writer or due to "diversities of inherited text," the various attempts at popular or learned expression in the interest of esoteric or of orthodox conviction. Further, we shall treat separately, and with modest intent as to detail (Appendix C), some relevant manuscript evidence from Codex D as well as selected *agrapha* in order to observe variations in the sayings of Jesus probably due to variations within the oral tradition. Material from apocryphal gospels and from other purportedly evangelic sources will be selectively examined with a view toward testing their claims as independent witnesses for the words of Jesus. More significantly, perhaps, we shall observe in this material, also, the ubiquitous operation of special interests competing for priority in the maturing life of the Christian church.

In the selection of quotations, we shall not ordinarily be concerned with allusions, "echoes," or "reminiscences," or with instances of incorporation of biblical passages within

[27] A. von Harnack, *The Origin of the New Testament*, trans. J. R. Wilkinson (New York, 1925), pp. 7f.

[28] Euseb., *H.E.* v.16. He hesitated to indict heresy with Scripture lest he seem presumptuously to supplement ($\pi\rho\circ\sigma\theta\epsilon\hat{\iota}\nu\alpha\iota$) or otherwise debase ($\dot{\alpha}\phi\epsilon\lambda\epsilon\hat{\iota}\nu$) the already perfectly expounded New Testament message.

the framework of a writer's own expression. Further, though
the formula λέγει Ἰησοῦς (Jesus says) or γέγραπται (it is
written) sometimes introduces highly questionable data,[29]
upon the authority of some such cue we may, by and large,
reasonably assume a responsible attempt at quotation.

Variants will be discussed within categories commonly
recognized by textual critics.[30] According to the motivation
prompting them, they will be seen to fall, for the most part,
under the following headings: Ethical and Practical, Explanatory, Stylistic, Dogmatic — along with such additional
orders to this classification as may emerge in the course of
investigation.[31]

---

[29] *The Epistle of Barnabas, passim*, and Justin Martyr represent in this
regard, to a somewhat higher degree, a type of error frequently to be met
with even later. Semisch, *Apostolischen Denkwurdikeiten des Martyrers
Justinus* (Hamburg und Gotha, 1848), p. 231, calls attention to the very
curious citation of Epiphanius (*Adv. haeres.* xlii.11) wherein he quotes the
so-called Apostolic Symbol as Scripture.

[30] Note especially R. P. Lagrange's excellent summary, p. 496.

[31] Scientific treatment of patristic quotations has, until comparatively
recent times, been hampered by the fact of defective transmission. So active
have been scribes in the correction of patristic texts to the later, or Byzantine,
standards with which they were familiar, that often, as Lake warns, less
importance attaches to a concordant than to a variant reading. Wherever
possible, however, reference has been made to patristic citations available in
Die Griechischen Christlichen Schriftsteller series. Nevertheless, with outstanding exceptions — as, for example, in the case of Sanday and Turner's
excellent edition of Irenaeus (*Novum Testamentum Sancti Irenaei*, Oxford,
1923) or Goodspeed's *Die ältesten Apologeten* (Göttingen, 1914) — we are
limited, as R. M. Grant notes, to the "necessary but unsatisfactory evidence
from old editions" until the completion of the Berlin Corpus (*New Testament Manuscript Studies*, Chicago, 1950, p. 119).

II

Prudential Motivation

In *The Peril of Modernizing Jesus*, Professor Cadbury discusses some of the motives to be observed in Jesus' teaching. Consistently to be met with are injunctions predicated solely on "self-regarding" or the simplest "prudential" considerations. Thus, for example, ready agreement with one's enemy in the way (Matthew v.25–26; Luke xii.58–59) is merely the exercise of a prudence calculated to preclude the "happening of a worse thing."

Under the heading "Prudential Motivation" at least two instances, both from the *Didache*, should be examined.

Didache 1.4

ἐὰν ἀγγαρεύσῃ σέ τις μίλιον ἕν, ὕπαγε μετ' αὐτοῦ δύο· ἐὰν ἄρῃ τις τὸ ἱμάτιόν σου, δὸς αὐτῷ καὶ τὸν χιτῶνα· ἐὰν λάβῃ τις ἀπὸ σοῦ τὸ σόν, μὴ ἀπαίτει· οὐδὲ γὰρ δύνασαι.[1]

Matthew v.40–42 (cf. Luke vi.29–30)

καὶ τῷ θέλοντί σοι κριθῆναι καὶ τὸν χιτῶνά σου λαβεῖν, ἄφες αὐτῷ καὶ τὸ ἱμάτιον· καὶ ὅστις σε ἀγγαρεύσει μίλιον ἕν, ὕπαγε μετ' αὐτοῦ δύο. τῷ αἰτοῦντί σε δός, καὶ τὸν θέλοντα ἀπὸ σοῦ δανίσασθαι μὴ ἀποστραφῇς.[2]

---

[1] "If any one forces you to go one mile, go with him two. If any man take your coat, give him your shirt also. If any man will take from you what is yours, do not refuse it, for neither are you able."

[2] ". . . and if any one would sue you and take your coat, let him have your cloak as well; and if any one forces you to go one mile, go with him

The similarity of the order of the gospel sentences in the
Didache at this point to that found in the *Diatessaron* of
Tatian has already been pointed out by Harnack. Inference
as to literary dependence, however, would seem to have no
material bearing on our present interest. For whether we
have here a blending of Matthew and Luke, the reproduction
of a source similar to the "Sayings" (Λόγια), the utilization
of a gospel harmony, or the echo of oral tradition, the homogeneity of these passages with Synoptic tradition is sufficient
to allow for comparison. At once, then, οὐδὲ γὰρ δύνασαι
(for neither are you able) meets the eye as a variant compatible with this category. Though the expression may be, as
Lake suggests, but a "flippant gloss," its purpose is evident
— a prompting to realistic appreciation of inalterable fact.
Lake's further suggestion that the original Greek, if recoverable, would probably read, "not even if you can," appears
unnecessary. Such refined emendation, it seems, takes too
little account of what Bishop Lightfoot rightly calls "the
archaic simplicity of the practical suggestions" so very characteristic of this document.

Didache i.3

ποία γὰρ χάρις, ἐὰν ἀγαπᾶτε τοὺς ἀγαπῶντας ὑμᾶς; οὐχὶ καὶ τὰ ἔθνη τὸ
αὐτὸ ποιοῦσιν; ὑμεῖς δὲ ἀγαπᾶτε τοὺς μισοῦντας ὑμᾶς, καὶ οὐχ ἕξετε
ἐχθρόν.[3]

Matthew v.44, 46

Ἐγὼ δὲ λέγω ὑμῖν, ἀγαπᾶτε τοὺς ἐχθροὺς ὑμῶν καὶ προσεύχεσθε ὑπὲρ
τῶν διωκόντων ὑμᾶς . . . ἐὰν γὰρ ἀγαπήσητε τοὺς ἀγαπῶντας ὑμᾶς,
τίνα μισθὸν ἔχετε; οὐχὶ καὶ οἱ τελῶναι τὸ αὐτὸ ποιοῦσιν; [4]

---

two miles. Give to him who begs from you, and do not refuse him who
would borrow from you."

[3] "For what credit is it to you if you love those that love you? Do not
even the heathen do the same? But you love those that hate you, and you
will not have an enemy."

[4] "But I say to you, Love your enemies and pray for those that persecute
you. For if you love those who love you, what reward have you? Do not
even the tax collectors do the same?"

Here the uncanonical sequence of verses is again noticeable and to this phenomenon the same critical observations apply. But attention is drawn particularly to the καὶ οὐχ ἕξετε ἐχθρόν (and you will not have an enemy), which the writer has seen fit to insert. And though the righteousness of "the Gentiles" is presumably to be exceeded, the sanctions lie rather in what is practically to be gained than in what is spiritually to be rendered.

III

Contextual Adaptation

In his *Kritische Untersuchungen über die Evangelien Justins*, Hilgenfeld has given a balanced statement of some of the possible headings under which many variants must be subsumed. He says, in part: "One must determine whether deviation among quotations is to be explained by the influence of context, by greater or less accuracy of citation, or finally by a difference of text." It is, of course, obvious that many additional categories might have been included in this summary appraisal of sources of unintentional variation.

Now surely loose citation bordering upon mere paraphrase may be reasonably dismissed as a substantial basis for critical textual comparison. And, to be sure, the phenomenon of textual peculiarities due to "diversities of inherited text" has, since Westcott and Hort, become as commonplace to the textual critic as it is complex. The challenge of Hilgenfeld's assertion therefore lies, for our purpose, in his recognition of context (*Zusammenhang*) as a determinative influence in the matter of textual change — change which this study proposes to relate to deliberate, purposive emendation.

It is to be remembered at the outset that the early Christians were not scrupulously concerned with the employment of a quotation in the spirit of its original setting. On the contrary, the use of a given passage of Scripture was deemed "profitable" in a wide and strange variety of circumstances.

This edification was achieved by means of a technique of quotation which made both detail and syntax subserve the purpose of context. In a very real sense, however, perhaps all variants, so far as they are not accidental, may be said to be adaptations to context. It may be conceded further that a quotation, however sketchy, has presumably had its basis in one or another of the several motives enumerated above. It does not nevertheless follow that, despite the absence of formal accuracy or completeness, such citations are necessarily to be identified as merely "loose and mnemonic" reproductions of text, though many may indeed be properly so labeled. For there is certainly the very plausible alternative that a number of such passages may be in fact consciously turned adaptations to context. Of such a possibility the following examples seem eminently suggestive.

Clement of Alexandria, *Stromata* v.11

μακάριοι τῷ ὄντι κατὰ τὴν γραφὴν οἱ πεινῶντες καὶ διψῶντες τὴν ἀλήθειαν, ὅτι πλησθήσονται τροφῆς ἀϊδίου.[1]

Matthew v.6

μακάριοι οἱ πεινῶντες καὶ διψῶντες τὴν δικαιοσύνην, ὅτι αὐτοὶ χορτασθήσονται.[2]

Arguing from philosophical premises, Clement here documents from Greek sources certain Gnostic principles and practices. The present context, therefore, is in defense of the assertion that "knowledge is the food of reason." And since the congenial goal of knowledge is truth, Clement makes bold to equate the concept "truth" (ἀλήθεια) with that of "righteousness" (δικαιοσύνη) in the interest of his context

---

[1] "Blessed truly are they, according to the scripture, who hunger and thirst for the truth, for they shall be filled with everlasting food."

[2] "Blessed are they who hunger and thirst for righteousness, for they shall be satisfied."

— τροφῆς ἀϊδίου (everlasting food) being a further adaptation of obviously explanatory character.

Irenaeus IV.xxx.3

*Facite vobis amicos de mammona iniquitatis, ut hi, quando fugati
fueritis, recipiant vos in aeterna tabernacula.*

Luke xvi.9

ἑαυτοῖς ποιήσατε φίλους ἐκ τοῦ μαμωνᾶ τῆς ἀδικίας, ἵνα ὅταν ἐκλίπῃ
δέξωνται ὑμᾶς εἰς τὰς αἰωνίους σκηνάς.[3]

Irenaeus' consistently accurate manner of quotation gives
rise to the suspicion that his variants are of set purpose. We
are at once attracted, therefore, by his *fugati fueritis*, which
is without textual or other documentary attestation. Irenaeus
is at this point expounding the analogy to be drawn between
the Israelites' flight from Egypt and the Christians' with-
drawal from the world. The canonical "fail" (ἐκλίπῃ), therefore, would have comported ill with the idea to be conveyed.
Fugati fueritis, however, afforded the effective accommodation to context here made.

From the two following quotations it is evident that
Clement of Alexandria was capable of reproducing the text
of Matthew v.28 with a fair degree of accuracy.

Stromata iii.14

πᾶς ὁ βλέπων γυναῖκα πρὸς τὸ ἐπιθυμῆσαι ἤδη ἐμοίχευσεν αὐτήν.[4]

Stromata iv.18

ἐγὼ δὲ λέγω, ὁ ἐμβλέψας τῇ γυναικὶ πρὸς ἐπιθυμίαν ἤδη μεμοίχευκεν.

---

[3] "Make friends for yourselves by means of unrighteous mammon, so
that when it fails, they may receive you into the eternal habitations."
[4] "Every one who looks at a woman lustfully has already committed
adultery with her."

Matthew v.28

Ἐγὼ δὲ λέγω ὑμῖν ὅτι πᾶς ὁ βλέπων γυναῖκα πρὸς τὸ ἐπιθυμῆσαι [αὐτὴν]
ἤδη ἐμοίχευσεν αὐτὴν ἐν τῇ καρδίᾳ αὐτοῦ.[5]

The following variations are therefore curious and, it seems,
relevant to the discussion of contextual adaptation.[6]

Stromata ii.11

ὁ ἰδὼν πρὸς ἐπιθυμίαν ἐμοίχευσεν.

Clement is here enjoining the true Gnostic to prepare his
faculties for the reception of the knowledge born only of
faith. To this end, he is to abstain from error either of speech,
thought, action, or of sensation (κατὰ αἴσθησιν). Under such
discipline, then, even the lustful look makes for sinful
defilement.

Stromata ii.14

ὁ ἐμβλέψας πρὸς ἐπιθυμίαν κρίνεται.

Clement's discussion has to do with the element of delib-
erateness or choice in the committing of sins or of torts. His
thesis is: that which involves choice involves judgment (Τὰ
προαιρετικὰ . . . κρίνεται). The voluntary look of lust, accordingly, is here liable to condemnatory judgment. Hence
his emendation of ἐμοίχευσεν to read κρίνεται.

Stromata ii.15

ὁ γὰρ ἐπιθυμήσας ἤδη μεμοίχευκε, φησίν.

[5] "But I say, every one who looks at a woman lustfully has already committed adultery with her in her heart."

[6] By reason of Clement of Alexandria's relatively free method of citation,
the possibility must never be dismissed that his quotations, however full,
have been given from memory. This fact obviously renders any attempt at
exact, scientific deduction on the basis of his text subject to critical re-
appraisal. It is because of his frequently fragmentary quotation, however,
that we may test par excellence the validity of the contextual principle here
suggested.

In development of his principle that the imputation of sin
turns about the factor of choice, Clement here calls attention to the element of willfulness inherent in the very act of
lusting. The judgment of sin (ἐμοίχευσεν) therefore logically
follows.

Clement of Alexandria, *Paedagogus* iii.5

ὁ γὰρ ἐμβλέψας, φησί, περιεργότερον ἤδη ἤμαρτεν.

In this chapter Clement is inveighing against the habit of
indecent exposure to which many women in his day were
given. And in an effort to obviate the lascivious glance, Clement, as though he would "build a fence" about the prohibition, upbraids even the curious look (περιεργότερον).

Clement of Alexandria, *Protrepticus* 10

οὐκ ἐπιθυμήσεις, ἐπιθυμίᾳ γὰρ μόνῃ μεμοίχευκας.

Clement, in this context, poses the option between God-
service and man-service. Whichever the choice, there are certain fundamental laws inexorably operative in either sphere.
God, the Christians' Lawgiver, Clement explains, has already
set forth certain ordinances. But these, the Ten Commandments, have been supplemented by even more recent divine
enactments: Thou shalt love thy neighbor as thyself; to him
who strikes thee on the cheek, offer also the other; thou
shalt not lust, and so forth. How much more effectual than
the prohibition, Clement concludes, are those injunctions
which anticipate the sinful act in the very desire. Matthew
v.28, therefore, he has thus happily adapted to the formal
arrangement of the new Decalogue.

It is difficult to believe that association of ideas or careless
quotation can account for the foregoing variants. It is perhaps safe also to assert that a *lapsus memoriae* cannot be

convincingly charged in the handling of a passage in the proportions of Matthew v.28 — at least not one so frequently dealt with as is evident.[7]

[7] The substance of this section appeared originally as an article in the *Journal of Biblical Literature*, LXVII (1948), 347–351.

IV

Harmonistic Motivation

Harmonizations, as might be expected, have found peculiarly extensive lodgment in the text of the New Testament. The principle of conformity and agreement, so far as scribes, editors, and revisers were concerned, was of the essence of dogma in the matter of scriptural relationships. Hence it is not strange that Jerome found harmonistic activity to be the principal cause of the disorder in Latin texts prior to his revision. Maurice Goguel [1] cites some fifteen instances of this kind of occurrence in the text of our Gospels, and this with the intention of being merely illustrative. In fact, so frequently are harmonistic glosses to be met with that von Soden has postulated the existence and widespread use of an early gospel harmony as alone sufficient to account for the phenomenon.

The point of importance for the present interest, however, is the purposeful, deliberate process of documentary selection and synthesis implied — whether in the literary activity of scribe or editor or in the fact of a gospel harmony — which is the basis of harmonization properly so called, or at least in its more significant manifestations. Only under these conditions, it would seem, would one be justified in speaking of "motivation" undergirding harmonization. For a method of quotation which makes consistent use of memory and of free

[1] Pp. 6off.

paraphrase cannot safely be depended upon to yield other than the kind of harmonization effected by the most casual and accidental association of ideas. Indeed, it is safe to assert that memory and the concomitant process of association of ideas may be made to account for most of the "harmonizations" to be found in the writings of both Justin and Tertullian. This would be generally true of nervous, polemical citation, making, as it does, large demands upon the ability of ready recall and placing a premium on suggestion and summary.

From Justin Martyr, for example, follow two such instances of questionable identification of harmonistic activity.[2]

Justin Martyr, *Apologia* i.15.10

Παντὶ τῷ αἰτοῦντι δίδοτε καὶ τὸν βουλόμενον δανείσασθαι μὴ ἀποστρα-
φῆτε. εἰ γὰρ δανείζετε παρ' ὧν ἐλπίζετε λαβεῖν, τί καινὸν ποιεῖτε; [3]

Matthew v.42, 46 (Luke vi.30)

Τῷ αἰτοῦντί σε δός, καὶ τὸν θέλοντα ἀπὸ σοῦ δανίσασθαι μὴ ἀποστραφῇς.
οὐχὶ καὶ οἱ τελῶναι τὸ αὐτὸ ποιοῦσιν;

Luke vi.34

καὶ ἐὰν δανίσητε παρ' ὧν ἐλπίζετε λαβεῖν, ποία ὑμῖν χάρις ἐστίν; [4]

Παντί (to everyone) is, of course, from the Lucan parallel, vi.30. Luke vi.34 is apparently the source out of which the idea of "lending" is enlarged. And Matthew v.46 thus furnishes an apt conclusion. Verbal differences in the quotation, however, over against both Matthean and Lucan sources,

---

[2] Cited by E. L. Titus, *ad loc.*

[3] "Give to every one who begs, and do not refuse him who would borrow. For if you lend to those from whom you hope to receive, what new thing are you doing?"

[4] "Give to him who begs from you, and do not refuse him who would borrow from you. Do not even the tax collectors do the same?" (Mt. v.42, 46). "And if you lend to those from whom you hope to receive, what credit is that to you?" (Lk. vi.34).

render it improbable that the present combination is due to
a studied association of texts. Further, oral tradition or gospel harmony would seem rather gratuitously suggested to
explain what is here felt to be more naturally accounted for
on other grounds. For it seems sufficient to assume that
canonical sources have been thus rendered *memoriter* and
that an easy association of cognate ideas most probably suggested the Lucan supplement. Again, Matthew v.46 appears
less by way of harmonization than as a readily conceived
term for this body of Synoptic thought.

Justin Martyr, *Dialogus* 112.4

Τάφοι κεκονιαμένοι, ἔξωθεν φαινόμενοι ὡραῖοι, καὶ ἔσωθεν γέμοντες ὀστέων νεκρῶν, τὸ ἡδύοσμον ἀποδεκατοῦντες, τὴν δὲ κάμηλον καταπίνοντες,
τυφλοὶ ὁδηγοί· [5]

Matthew xxiii.27

Οὐαὶ ὑμῖν, γραμματεῖς καὶ Φαρισαῖοι ὑποκριταί, ὅτι παρομοιάζετε τάφοις
κεκονιαμένοις, οἵτινες ἔξωθεν μὲν φαίνονται ὡραῖοι ἔσωθεν δὲ γέμουσιν
ὀστέων νεκρῶν καὶ πάσης ἀκαθαρσίας·

Matthew xxiii.23–24

ἀποδεκατοῦτε τὸ ἡδύοσμον καὶ τὸ ἄνηθον καὶ τὸ κύμινον . . . διυλίζοντες
τὸν κώνωπα τὴν δὲ κάμηλον καταπίνοντες.[6]

It seems quite probable that we have to do with but a
summary framework embracing instances of typical pharisaic
misplacement of ethical emphasis, according to Justin's context, and not with a purposefully conceived aggregation of
harmonistic texts.

[5] "Whitewashed tombs, which appear outwardly beautiful, and within are
full of dead men's bones, tithing mint and swallowing a camel, you blind
guides!"
[6] "Woe to you, scribes and Pharisees, hypocrites! for you are like whitewashed tombs, which outwardly appear beautiful, but within are full of
dead men's bones and all uncleanness" (xxiii.27). "For you tithe mint and dill
and cummin . . . straining out a gnat and swallowing a camel!" (xxiii.23–24).

It is because of method of quotation, therefore, that it would seem precarious to instance this category from other than those writers whose literary references are observed to be of a certain approved level of accuracy. Irenaeus, for example, might furnish a valid source for an examination of harmonistic interests.

Irenaeus V.xxxiii.1

Hic est sanguis meus novi testamenti, qui pro multis effundetur in remissionem peccatorum.

Matthew xxvi.28

Τοῦτο γάρ ἐστιν τὸ αἷμά μου τῆς διαθήκης τὸ περὶ πολλῶν ἐκχυννόμενον εἰς ἄφεσιν ἁμαρτιῶν.[7]

Luke xxii.20

Τοῦτο τὸ ποτήριον ἡ καινὴ διαθήκη ἐν τῷ αἵματί μου, τὸ ὑπὲρ ὑμῶν ἐκχυννόμενον.[8]

Harmonization, the insertion of the attribute *novi* to accompany *testamenti*, may be accounted for equally well by the ascription of motivation to Irenaeus as to his source. A C D W Old Syriac preserve this reading which Neutral authorities omit. Certainly, however, Irenaeus' own emphasis upon the progressive work of salvation mediated through the Testaments is in keeping with the reading recorded. If, on the other hand, harmonization may be assumed (and it is difficult to see how the Neutral could be here the emended text), the assimilation of a Matthean model to Lucan details is evident — a change, quite probably, originating in Irenaeus' source.

---

[7] "For this is my blood of the covenant, which is poured out for many for the forgiveness of sins."

[8] "This cup which is poured out for you is the new covenant in my blood."

Irenaeus IV.viii.1

*Quoniam venient ab oriente et ab occidente, ab aquilone et ab
austro, et recumbent cum Abraham et Isaac et Jacob in regno
caelorum.*

Matthew viii.11

λέγω δὲ ὑμῖν ὅτι πολλοὶ ἀπὸ ἀνατολῶν καὶ δυσμῶν ἥξουσιν καὶ ἀνακλι-
θήσονται μετὰ Ἀβραὰμ καὶ Ἰσαὰκ καὶ Ἰακὼβ ἐν τῇ βασιλείᾳ τῶν
οὐρανῶν· [9]

Luke xiii.29

καὶ ἥξουσιν ἀπὸ ἀνατολῶν καὶ δυσμῶν καὶ ἀπὸ βορρᾶ καὶ νότου κτλ.[10]

The universality of the salvation which is to be the inheritance of Abraham's seed is expressed in unequivocal terms
as Luke xiii.29 is drawn upon to reinforce in the fullest geo-
graphical proportions the Matthean apocalyptic setting —
a supplement scarcely accidental in view of the demands of
Irenaeus' argument.

Irenaeus IV.xxix.1

*Vestri autem beati oculi, qui vident quae videtis, et aures vestrae,
quae audiunt quae auditis.*

Matthew xiii.16–17

ὑμῶν δὲ μακάριοι οἱ ὀφθαλμοὶ ὅτι βλέπουσιν, καὶ τὰ ὦτα [ὑμῶν] ὅτι
ἀκούουσιν . . . πολλοὶ . . . ἐπεθύμησαν ἰδεῖν ἃ βλέπετε . . . καὶ
ἀκοῦσαι ἃ ἀκούετε.[11]

---

[9] "I tell you, many will come from east and west and sit at table with
Abraham, Isaac, and Jacob in the kingdom of heaven."

[10] "And men will come from east and west and from north and south, etc."

[11] "But blessed are your eyes, for they see, and your ears, for they hear . . .
many . . . longed to see what you see . . . and to hear what you hear."

Luke x.23–24

Μακάριοι οἱ ὀφθαλμοὶ οἱ βλέποντες ἃ βλέπετε . . . πολλοὶ . . .
ἠθέλησαν ἰδεῖν ἃ ὑμεῖς βλέπετε κτλ.[12]

There is a reasonable presumption that Irenaeus has thus
effected consciously a blending of the Matthean and Lucan
parallels set forth. Indeed, the clauses "quae videtis, et
. . . quae auditis" give a sort of homiletic completeness
to the Matthean framework with a purpose apparently explanatory in the light of the context.

[12] "Blessed are the eyes which see what you see! . . . many desired to see
what you see, etc."

V

Stylistic Motivation

The same spirit of caution must be exercised in assessing instances to be subsumed under the heading "Stylistic Motivation" as seemed necessary in discussing the harmonistic gloss. Again we must inquire whether in the occurrences to be considered the variant may be accounted for on the basis of an intentional preoccupation as to style or whether it is a mere by-product of some more fundamental interest. It seems proper to assert that in a canvassing of patristic literature for manifestations of stylistic concern, a distinction ought boldly to be made between reviser and polemicist, editor and homilist. Although the distinction may not be decisive, it is at least a significant one which emphasizes the differences in degree of interest in matters of style reasonably to be expected of these two groups.

In similar vein, Norden poses an important consideration relevant to the discussion of this category. In an incisive contrast between early Christian and classical literature, he cites the freedom and the individualistic quality of pagan writings as over against a kind of "corporate compactness" attaching to Christian literary productions. High importance must be placed in this contrast, continues Norden, upon the literary self-consciousness of the one (*exegi monumentum*) [1] and the

---

[1] *Die antike Kunstprosa* (2 vols.; Leipzig, 1898), II, 454–456.

over-arching authority which is the constant factor in the
thinking of the other ("for it is not you who speak, but the
Holy Spirit"). In short, the antithesis is one of form versus
content. Nevertheless, inevitably, second-century Christian
writers, according to their interests and culture, found on
occasion more congenial expression in studied choice than in
ordinary acceptance of terms. Yet we should be prepared,
in the nature of these and of other limitations to be observed,
to understate rather than to exaggerate our case.

Justin Martyr, *Apologia* i.15.16

ὅπου γὰρ ὁ θησαυρός ἐστιν, ἐκεῖ καὶ ὁ νοῦς τοῦ ἀνθρώπου.[2]

Matthew vi.21 (Luke xii.34)

ὅπου γάρ ἐστιν ὁ θησαυρός σου, ἐκεῖ ἔσται καὶ ἡ καρδία σου.[3]

Clement of Alexandria, too, quotes this passage and with
the identical variation — ὁ νοῦς τοῦ ἀνθρώπου (the mind of
man). The quasi-philosophical turn thus given the quotation
represents appropriately the interests of both Clement and
Justin. Certainly the change serves, in the words of Lagrange,
"pour rendre le texte — d'origine sémitique indirecte — plus
accessible aux Grecs. . ." There seems, then, little doubt of
the stylistic improvement thus sought.

Clement of Alexandria, *Paedagogus* i.11

ὁ γὰρ ἀγαθὸς ποιμὴν τὴν ψυχὴν ἑαυτοῦ τίθησιν ὑπὲρ τῶν προβάτων.[4]

John x.11

ὁ ποιμὴν ὁ καλὸς τὴν ψυχὴν αὐτοῦ τίθησιν ὑπὲρ τῶν προβάτων.[5]

[2] "For where his treasure is, there also is the mind of man." Cf. *Strom.* v.11
(p. 19).
[3] "For where your treasure is, there will your heart be also."
[4] "For the good shepherd lays down his life for the sheep."
[5] Similarly rendered.

P. M. Barnard [6] calls attention to Clement's consistent use
of ἀγαθός (good) in this quotation (six times) as against a
single occurrence of καλός, the correct reading. To be sure,
according to Vincent,[7] classical usage reserved καλός for the
description of outward form. On the other hand, ἀγαθός as
a moral attribute (frequently so applied, as Liddell and Scott
point out, by the philosophical writers after Plato) was more
apt to commend itself to Clement as being stylistically pref-
erable on the basis of the philosophical distinctions implied.

Clement of Alexandria, *Stromata* vii.14

Ὅ τε γὰρ θεὸς ἐπὶ δικαίους καὶ ἀδίκους τὸν αὐτοῦ ἐπιλάμπει ἥλιον.[8]

Matthew v.45

ὅτι τὸν ἥλιον αὐτοῦ ἀνατέλλει ἐπὶ πονηροὺς καὶ ἀγαθοὺς καὶ βρέχει
ἐπὶ δικαίους καὶ ἀδίκους.[9]

Barnard notices also that Clement of Alexandria five times
substitutes ἐπιλάμπει for ἀνατέλλει, although elsewhere
(*Paedagogus* i.9) he manifests an acquaintance with the
correct reading. If, therefore, stylistic improvement is here
intended, as seems likely, Clement, in enlarging upon the
idea of the sunrise (ἀνατέλλει), suggests more eloquently by
his change the continuous outpouring upon mankind of divine
love and light. Such an intention seems amply substantiated
by the context.

[6] *The Biblical Text of Clement of Alexandria, Texts and Studies,* V, 2
(Cambridge, England, 1899), p. 59 n.

[7] *Word Studies in the New Testament* (2 vols.; New York, 1899), I, 190.

[8] "For God makes his sun shine on the just and on the unjust."

[9] "For he makes his sun rise on the evil and on the good and sends rain on
the just and on the unjust."

Clement of Alexandria, *Quis Dives Salvetur* 4

εὐκόλως διὰ τῆς τρυμαλιᾶς τῆς βελόνης κάμηλος εἰσελεύσεται ἢ πλούσιος
εἰς τὴν βασιλείαν τοῦ θεοῦ.[10]

Mark x.25

εὐκοπώτερόν ἐστιν κάμηλον διὰ τρυμαλιᾶς ῥαφίδος διελθεῖν ἢ πλούσιον
εἰς τὴν βασιλείαν τοῦ θεοῦ εἰσελθεῖν.[11]

Here Clement announces his quotation of the text of
Mark.[12] For our purpose, attention turns about the use of
βελόνης (needle) for the grammatically stigmatized ῥαφίδος
(εὐκόλως being, as Barnard thinks, an obvious error, probably for εὐκοπώτερον). Quoting at some length, at this point,
Clement is probably quoting from a text. The use of βελόνης
is thus the more noticeable; though previously (*Q.D.S.* 2)
when quoting the same passage, he curiously uses ῥαφίδος.
Yet a third and final use of this verse by Clement (*Q.D.S.*
26) shows βελόνης. Although this latter instance is possibly
a quotation of Luke xviii.25, it is presumably a further
demonstration from the Marcan text and so suggests, if
it does not confirm, nonaccidental variation on stylistic
grounds.

Tertullian, *Adversus Praxean* 22

*Tunc, inquit, cognoscetis quod ego sim et a memetipso nihil loquar,
sed sicut me docuit, ita et loquor . . .*

[10] "More easily shall a camel enter through the eye of a needle than a rich
man into the kingdom of God."

[11] Similarly rendered except for use of the present tense.

[12] This is important. For example, Titus concludes from Clement's use of
σκίμποδα (*Paed.* i.2) that we are in possession of a "stylistic" variation. But
σκίμποδα might be as well a ready sense variant for either κλίνην (Mt. ix.6)
or for κλινίδιον (Lk. v.24) as an improvement of the admittedly inelegant
κράβαττον.

John viii.28

τότε γνώσεσθε ὅτι ἐγώ εἰμι, καὶ ἀπ' ἐμαυτοῦ ποιῶ οὐδέν, ἀλλὰ καθὼς
ἐδίδαξέν με ὁ πατὴρ ταῦτα λαλῶ.[13]

In the three examples from *Adversus Praxean* we shall
see what seems to be a series of corrections according to
sense. In this tractate Tertullian has drawn heavily upon the
Gospel of John. In all probability, therefore, he is, especially
in the longer passages, referring to a text. But it happens that
the instances here set forth are shorter excerpts and could
possibly have been quoted from memory. For impressive is
the fact that the "corrections" to which attention is called
deal with passages upon which certain logical necessities of
speech would have made demands in the process of mnemonic
quotation; though they could equally have influenced a writer
in the process of deliberate stylistic emendation. On the other
hand, verbal correspondences between the Latin and the
Greek, in addition to the consecutive references to the Gospel, make it probable that we are here dealing with a more
careful treatment of the text than that which Tertullian is
wont to give.

It is to be noted that in this instance, for example, Tertullian has effected a logical balance of ideas revolving about
sicut me docuit by means of the substitution of "speaking"
for "doing." It is at once interesting to observe here the applicability of the alternative considerations suggested above.

Adversus Praxean 22

*Ego, inquit, quae vidi penes patrem meum loquor, et vos quod
vidistis penes patrem vestrum, id facitis.*

---

[13] "Then you will know that I am he, and that I do nothing on my own
authority but speak thus as the Father taught me."

John viii.38

ἃ ἐγὼ ἑώρακα παρὰ τῷ πατρὶ λαλῶ· καὶ ὑμεῖς οὖν ἃ ἠκούσατε παρὰ τοῦ πατρὸς ποιεῖτε.[14]

Tertullian is apparently again, in this passage, decided by logical parallels suggested by the context. Both the "speaking" and the "doing," he would seem to reason, are conditioned by what each party has seen of his father — a parallelism apparently broken down by the text, where "speaking" and "seeing," "doing" and "hearing" have been equated less happily.

Adversus Praxean 22

Loquor, inquit, vobis et non creditis. Opera quae ego facio in nomine patris, ipsa de me testimonium dicunt.

John x.25

Εἶπον ὑμῖν καὶ οὐ πιστεύετε· τὰ ἔργα ἃ ἐγὼ ποιῶ ἐν τῷ ὀνόματι τοῦ πατρός μου ταῦτα μαρτυρεῖ περὶ ἐμοῦ.[15]

Both Christ's performance of his works and the corresponding witness thereby borne of him obtain in the present. Similarly, therefore, the exhortation and the unbelief. Some such verbal accommodation Tertullian has quite probably intended in the interest of style.[16]

[14] "I speak of what I have seen with my Father, and you do what you have heard from your father."

[15] "I told you, and you do not believe. The works that I do in my Father's name, they bear witness to me."

[16] For occurrences of a similar accommodation, principally of a circumstantial kind, see Iren. V.xxxiii.1, where *effundetur* (Mt. xxvi.28) is read for ἐκχυννόμενον; and again (II.xx.5), where *tradetur* (Mt. xxiv.26) appears for παραδίδοται.

VI

Explanatory Motivation

Since the words of Jesus were not only normative for the good life but were themselves "spirit" and "life," both preacher and teacher were at great pains to make available their clear meaning to the laity. Allegorical interpretation mediated the hard sayings of the Old Testament to Christian apprehension. The explanatory gloss, while not quite so spectacular a device, served a kindred purpose by way of insertion or of appendage to dominical pronouncements.

To be sure, the motivation labeled "explanatory" is itself "ethical and practical" and religious in the widest sense. It is only that its function may be clearly seen for what it is worth that separate treatment is thus given.

Didache xvi.1

Γρηγορεῖτε ὑπὲρ τῆς ζωῆς ὑμῶν . . . οὐ γὰρ οἴδατε τὴν ὥραν, ἐν ᾗ ὁ κύριος ἡμῶν ἔρχεται.[1]

Matthew xxiv.42

γρηγορεῖτε οὖν, ὅτι οὐκ οἴδατε ποίᾳ ἡμέρᾳ ὁ κύριος ὑμῶν ἔρχεται.[2]

---

[1] "Watch over your life . . . for you do not know the hour in which our Lord is coming."

[2] "Watch, therefore, for you do not know on what day your Lord is coming."

It is not strange that a manual which purported to serve as a popular handbook for Christian living should have been pointed and unequivocal in every detail. Whereas, therefore, the apocalyptic γρηγορεῖτε (watch!) possessed of itself authoritative and urgent overtones, the interpolated ὑπὲρ τῆς ζωῆς ὑμῶν (over your life) added a prior and personal immediacy to its warning. This warning was now not only in reference to some future assize, but also concerned itself minutely with the details of daily living. Some such explanatory intent seems reasonably implied.

Justin Martyr, *Apologia* i.15.1

ὃς ἂν ἐμβλέψῃ γυναικὶ πρὸς τὸ ἐπιθυμῆσαι αὐτῆς ἤδη ἐμοίχευσε τῇ καρδίᾳ παρὰ τῷ θεῷ.[3]

Matthew v.28

πᾶς ὁ βλέπων γυναῖκα πρὸς τὸ ἐπιθυμῆσαι αὐτὴν ἤδη ἐμοίχευσεν αὐτὴν ἐν τῇ καρδίᾳ αὐτοῦ.[4]

The added παρὰ τῷ θεῷ (with God) leaves no doubt of the difficulty which Justin felt as to the practical value of this verse for ethical purposes. Certainly a pagan audience would have been unconvinced by the teaching as it stood. Hence the necessity of buttressing the already explanatory ἐν τῇ καρδίᾳ (in his heart) with the complementary παρὰ τῷ θεῷ, suggesting a dimension of ethical sanction and judgment beyond challenge.

Clement of Alexandria, *Paedagogus* ii.8

ὁ λαὸς οὗτος τοῖς χείλεσι φιλοῦσί με, ἡ δὲ καρδία αὐτῶν πορρωτέρω ἐστὶν ἀπ' ἐμοῦ.[5]

---

[3] "Whoever looks at a woman lustfully has already committed adultery with her before God."

[4] See note 5, Chapter III.

[5] "This people love me with their lips, but their heart is far from me."

Matthew xv.8 (Mark vii.6)

'Ο λαὸς οὗτος τοῖς χείλεσίν με τιμᾷ, ἡ δὲ καρδία αὐτῶν πόρρω ἀπέχει ἀπ' ἐμοῦ.[6]

It is to be inferred from the context that Clement is seeking to establish a mystical relationship between the traitorous kiss of Judas (φίλημα), which is his point of interest for the moment, and the deeper meaning of the Scripture here quoted. Thus it is evident that the indictment of lip-service (ὁ λαὸς οὗτος τοῖς χείλεσι φιλοῦσί με κτλ) is only now read in its proper setting. It is probable, however, that a reading involving "love" might have been available to Clement in his source. In fact, the Marcan parallel reads ἀγαπᾷ in D W a b c.[7] Yet Clement's own use of ἀγαπῶν elsewhere[8] serves merely to bring into stronger relief this unique occurrence of φιλοῦσι, an emendation conceived presumably for reasons of interpretation as indicated.

Clement of Alexandria, *Quis Dives Salvetur* 17

μακάριοι οἱ πεινῶντες καὶ διψῶντες τὴν δικαιοσύνην τοῦ θεοῦ.[9]

Matthew v.6

μακάριοι οἱ πεινῶντες καὶ διψῶντες τὴν δικαιοσύνην.[10]

Although there is no textual evidence for Clement's τοῦ θεοῦ, his observations at this point are suggestive. In the course of a somewhat analytical demonstration he asserts: "Wherefore also Matthew added, 'Blessed are the poor.' How? 'In spirit.' And again, 'Blessed are they that hunger

---

[6] "This people honors me with their lips, but their heart is far from me."

[7] Barnard (p. 19 n.), in fact, notes the closer similarity of Clement's readings on Mt. xv.8 to the Marcan text (Mk. vii.6).

[8] *Strom.* iv.7, 18.

[9] "Blessed are they who hunger and thirst for the righteousness of God."

[10] See note 2, Chapter III.

and thirst after the righteousness of God [τοῦ θεοῦ].' " It is, of course, possible that the "addition" in this instance assigned to the text of Matthew, Clement intended to refer only to δικαιοσύνην — τοῦ θεοῦ representing Clement's own intention further to sharpen the distinction. Nevertheless, whether to be related to the Matthean text or to Clement himself, the words were subjoined very likely with explanatory intent. Whether, too, the quarrel is with pharisaic or with any other sectarian definition of righteousness Clement does not intimate. In any case, the term, coupled with the instructive τοῦ θεοῦ, suggests a unique and definitive area of religious expression.

Irenaeus IV.xxxvi.3

Quomodo enim factum est in diebus Noe: manducabant at bibebant, et emebant et vendebant, nubebant et nubebantur, et non scierunt, quoadusque intravit Noe in arcam. . .

Luke xvii.26–27

καὶ καθὼς ἐγένετο ἐν ταῖς ἡμέραις Νῶε . . . ἤσθιον, ἔπινον, ἐγάμουν, ἐγαμίζοντο ἄχρι ἧς ἡμέρας εἰσῆλθεν Νῶε εἰς τὴν κιβωτόν.[11]

The point of interest in Irenaeus' quotation is, of course, the interposed *et non scierunt*. The worldly traffic of Sodom — the buying, the selling, and the like — had its fatal issue because the men of Sodom did not know, as it were, the hour of their visitation. Irenaeus therefore concludes this portion from Luke with the significant warning from Matthew (xxiv.42): "Vigilate igitur, quoniam nescitis qua die Dominus vester veniat." A further elaboration on this theme in the development of his argument makes reasonably clear the explanatory purpose which Irenaeus, quite probably, intended his gloss to serve.

[11] "And as it was in the days of Noah . . . they ate, they drank, they married, they were given in marriage until the day when Noah entered the ark."

Tertullian, *De Patientia* 13

Spiritus promptus, sed caro sine patientia infirma.

Matthew xxvi.41 (Mark xiv.38)

τὸ μὲν πνεῦμα πρόθυμον, ἡ δὲ σὰρξ ἀσθενής.[12]

There seems little doubt as to Tertullian's motivation in his insertion of *sine patientia* among the words of Jesus. For the inveterate conflict between flesh and spirit is projected on a cosmic plane, and the tenor of the entire essay is to explain the reconciliation to be achieved through the constant exercise of this now indispensable virtue.

Tertullian, *De Monogamia* 9

Unus ex passeribus duobus non cadit in terram sine patris voluntate.

Matthew x.29

οὐχὶ δύο στρουθία ἀσσαρίου πωλεῖται; καὶ ἓν ἐξ αὐτῶν οὐ πεσεῖται ἐπὶ τὴν γῆν ἄνευ τοῦ πατρὸς ὑμῶν.[13]

Textually, there is no available attestation for the *sine patris voluntate* recorded here. But the fact that the Latin Irenaeus (II.xxvi.2) presents the same reading implies that such a variant originated neither with Tertullian nor with Irenaeus but was possibly derived from their sources. In fact, the indifference of this reading to Irenaeus' argument renders this supposition probable. On the other hand, the emendation dispenses with the vague suggestiveness of the ordinary text and sponsors clearly a concept of divine governance admirably apposite to Tertullian's purpose. Thus,

---

[12] "The spirit indeed is willing, but the flesh is weak."

[13] "Are not two sparrows sold for a penny? And not one of them will fall to the ground without your Father."

though the reading reflects a dogmatic interest, the expression of this interest seems unmistakably explanatory.

Tertullian, *De Cultu Feminarum* 13

Luceant opera vestra.

Matthew v.16

οὕτως λαμψάτω τὸ φῶς ὑμῶν ἔμπροσθεν τῶν ἀνθρώπων, ὅπως ἴδωσιν ὑμῶν τὰ καλὰ ἔργα καὶ δοξάσωσιν τὸν πατέρα ὑμῶν . . .[14]

This reading apparently represents more than a hasty or arbitrary abridgment of Matthew v.16 on the part of Tertullian. For Tertullian elsewhere, Justin Martyr, and Clement of Alexandria [15] employ the same quotation. Such coincidence does, of course, suggest a documentary basis. Nevertheless, equally attractive is the possibility that we are here in possession of an oral version of Matthew v.16 available to these writers.

In each instance, the explanatory motivation underlying the epitome seems clearly set forth by Tertullian (*ad loc.*) in the declaration: "Haec sunt, quae nos luminaria mundi faciunt, bona scilicet nostra."

Ignatius, *Ad Polycarpum* ii.2

φρόνιμος γίνου ὡς ὄφις ἐν ἅπασιν καὶ ἀκέραιος εἰς ἀεὶ ὡς ἡ περιστερά.[16]

Matthew x.16

γίνεσθε οὖν φρόνιμοι ὡς οἱ ὄφεις καὶ ἀκέραιοι ὡς αἱ περιστεραί.[17]

One would not ordinarily appeal to the writings of Ignatius for a listing of intentionally conceived variants. The martyr

---

[14] "Let your light so shine before men, that they may see your good works and give glory to your Father," etc.

[15] *Idol.* 15, *Apol.* i.16, *Strom.* iii.4, iv.26, respectively.

[16] "Be wise as a serpent in all things and innocent as a dove forever."

[17] "Be wise as serpents and innocent as doves."

en route to execution would concern himself with but the
communication of his profoundest and most urgent impres-
sions in any oral or literary expression of farewell. Others
might more fittingly busy themselves in matters of exact
detail. Noteworthy, therefore, is the intensity of Ignatius'
style as it is reflected in this readily identified quotation from
Matthew. Nevertheless, to view his sweeping "in all things"
(ἐν ἅπασιν) and "forever" (εἰς ἀεί) as simply explanatory
agents is probably to miss the total effect which Ignatius was
attempting thus to achieve. For perhaps the uncompromising
conformity so rigorously urged is rather to be pondered than
explained.

VII

Ethical and Practical Motivation [1]

It is evident in the nature of the literature with which we are concerned that a category embracing variants of an ethical and practical character must necessarily bulk large. For it was inevitable that the interests of the second-century writers under our survey — moralists, teachers, preachers — should have been focussed primarily on some such area. Not only were the ordinary principles and observances of Christian morality to be studiously inculcated; but the details of one's personal habits and domestic responsibilities were to be regimented as matters no less weighty. In very truth, these men were literally concerned with the "perfecting of the saints" "in all things" and "forever." This they sought scrupulously to accomplish by what was considered a judicious adaptation of Scripture according to given circumstances.

It has seemed advisable to segregate the instances to be discussed according to certain dominant interests within the sphere of ethical and practical participation. These arbitrary subdivisions, however, are more methodological than real. They grow simply out of an attempt to illustrate trends in what might be otherwise but a series of loosely related occurrences.

[1] For this heading the author is indebted to E. L. Titus.

We shall treat first a group of variants involving relatively elemental ethical considerations.

Didache i.4

ἐάν τίς σοι δῷ ῥάπισμα εἰς τὴν δεξιὰν σιαγόνα, στρέψον αὐτῷ καὶ τὴν ἄλλην, καὶ ἔσῃ τέλειος.[2]

Matthew v.39

ὅστις σε ῥαπίζει εἰς τὴν δεξιὰν σιαγόνα σου, στρέψον αὐτῷ καὶ τὴν ἄλλην.[3]

It is, of course, instructive to note the attempt to define with authority maximal and minimal ethical requirements for a youthful Christian community. Although this summary of "perfection" (further enlarged) selects some of the more difficult pronouncements in the teaching of Jesus, interestingly enough, the standards thus set up are not final. For whereas a particular merit attaches to the man who "bears the entire yoke of the Lord," justification attends him also who "does what he can." Hence it is perhaps rather in the fact of the sufferance which it extends than of the exactions which it imposes that the ethical temper of this document is properly to be judged.

Justin Martyr, Apologia i.16.10

ὃς γὰρ ἀκούει μου καὶ ποιεῖ ἃ λέγω ἀκούει τοῦ ἀποστείλαντός με.[4]

Luke x.16 (cf. Matthew x.40, vii.24)

Ὁ ἀκούων ὑμῶν ἐμοῦ ἀκούει, καὶ ὁ ἀθετῶν ὑμᾶς ἐμὲ ἀθετεῖ· ὁ δὲ ἐμὲ ἀθετῶν ἀθετεῖ τὸν ἀποστείλαντά με.[5]

---

[2] "If any one strike you on the right cheek, turn to him the other also, and you will be perfect."

[3] "If any one strikes you on the right cheek, turn to him the other also."

[4] "He who hears me and does what I say hears him who sent me."

[5] "He who hears you hears me, and he who rejects you rejects me; and he who rejects me rejects him who sent me."

Tertullian, *Adversus Marcionem* iv.19 [6]

Quae mihi mater et qui mihi fratres? subiungens: nisi qui audiunt verba mea et faciunt ea.

Matthew xii.48,50 (cf. Luke viii.21)

Τίς ἐστιν ἡ μήτηρ μου, καὶ τίνες εἰσὶν οἱ ἀδελφοί μου; . . . ὅστις γὰρ ἂν ποιήσῃ τὸ θέλημα τοῦ πατρός μου τοῦ ἐν οὐρανοῖς. . .[7]

The similarity of these two quotations, turning about "hearing and doing," makes for their convenient consideration jointly. In each instance, the presence of the uncanonical "doing" and "hearing," respectively, may be accounted for by way of unconscious harmonization with a passage like Matthew vii.24, where the two functions are juxtaposed. In both citations, the emphasis effected by way of such supplement is in the interest of a more exact and a more binding definition of ethical and practical presuppositions. Indeed, the stress thus laid upon the priority of good works is a characteristic feature of the literature of the second century.

Quite apart from simple statements of ethical obligation, there are also to be detected within this order emendations offered with bluntly rigoristic intent.

Clement of Alexandria, *Stromata* vii.12

ἐὰν μὴ μισήσητε τὸν πατέρα καὶ τὴν μητέρα, πρὸς ἔτι δὲ καὶ τὴν ἰδίαν ψυχήν, καὶ ἐὰν μὴ τὸ σημεῖον βαστάσητε. . .[8]

[6] This quotation has been discussed in Appendix B as an alleged reading of Marcion's, but without reference to the present interest.

[7] "Who is my mother, and who are my brothers? . . . For whoever does the will of my Father in heaven," etc.

[8] "Unless you hate father and mother and even your own life, and unless you bear the sign [of the cross]," etc.

Luke xiv. 26–27

Εἴ τις ἔρχεται πρός με καὶ οὐ μισεῖ τὸν πατέρα ἑαυτοῦ καὶ τὴν μητέρα
. . . ἔτι τε καὶ τὴν ψυχὴν ἑαυτοῦ, οὐ δύναται εἶναί μου μαθητής. ὅστις
οὐ βαστάζει τὸν σταυρὸν ἑαυτοῦ. . .[9]

In a context which emphasizes the dichotomy of flesh and
spirit, Clement presents this quotation, in which the "bearing of the sign" ("of the cross" being understood, presumably) is the new and distinctive element. The ideal state of
Christian achievement, the state of Gnostic contemplation,
is here described in terms of rigidly ascetic renunciation.
For what is it "to bear the sign [of the cross]" but "to carry
about death, taking leave of all things while still alive"?

Stromata ii.5

πᾶς μὲν οὖν ὁ ποιῶν τὴν ἁμαρτίαν δοῦλός ἐστιν.[10]

John viii.34

πᾶς ὁ ποιῶν τὴν ἁμαρτίαν δοῦλός ἐστιν τῆς ἁμαρτίας.[11]

It is to be observed that Clement is probably here quoting
from his source, there being at this point Neutral-Western
alignments with reference to the inclusion or omission of "of
sin" (τῆς ἁμαρτίας). B C T L include, D b Sinaitic Syriac
omit these words. Clement's citation of this verse elewhere [12]
reveals a similar, shall we say, "noninterpolation." Thus,
while it is here questionable to speak of rigoristic emendation by the hand of Clement of Alexandria, such a reading
(from whatever source) derives certainly from a viewpoint

---

[9] "If any one comes to me and does not hate his own father and mother
. . . and even his own life, he cannot be my disciple. . . Whoever does not
bear his own cross," etc.
[10] "Every one who commits sin is a slave."
[11] "Every one who commits sin is a slave to sin."
[12] *Strom.* iii.4.

devoid of ethical compromise. In his inveighing against morbid perversions, Clement uses this sentiment effectively by way of wholesome Christian contrast.

Tertullian, *De Idolatria* 12

Nemo aratro manum imponens et retro spectans aptus est operi.

Luke ix.62

Οὐδεὶς ἐπιβαλὼν τὴν χεῖρα ἐπ' ἄροτρον καὶ βλέπων εἰς τὰ ὀπίσω εὔθετός ἐστιν τῇ βασιλείᾳ τοῦ θεοῦ.[13]

It is difficult to discern the meaning intended in Tertullian's substitution, *aptus operi*. One may perhaps even challenge its strict applicability. For whereas it is possible to spiritualize the nature of the "work" here mentioned, it is highly improbable that one would have sought improvement by means of the displacement of "the kingdom of God." Since, however, the quotation follows upon the assertion "sed filiis et posteritati providendum," is it possible that Tertullian means to declare that spiritual defection disqualifies, not only for entrance into the Kingdom of God, but for any wholesome earthly participation? Such spiritual dislocation is nevertheless the result of membership in a variety of trades and professions, against which, because of their direct or indirect support of idolatry, Tertullian argues vigorously. Less, then, in the judgment thus pronounced than in the offenses so minutely selected is the hand of the rigorist clearly perceived.

There are occasions when some special interest is brought into prominence and the consequent changes bear this particularistic coloring, so to say. Again Clement of Alexandria and Tertullian illustrate this process.

[13] "No one who puts his hand to the plough and looks back is fit for the kingdom of God."

Clement of Alexandria, *Paedagogus* iii.3

οὐδεὶς δὲ ἄλλος, φησὶν ὁ κύριος, δύναται ποιῆσαι τρίχα λευκὴν ἢ μέλαιναν.[14]

Tertullian, *De Cultu Feminarum* 6

Dominus ait: Quis vestrum potest capillum atrum ex albo facere aut album ex atro?

Matthew v.36

μήτε ἐν τῇ κεφαλῇ σου ὀμόσῃς, ὅτι οὐ δύνασαι μίαν τρίχα λευκὴν ποιῆσαι ἢ μέλαιναν.[15]

That the original context is not observed is, of course, not exceptional. Surely the adaptation of Matthew v.36 to apply against dyeing the hair is the part rather of originality than of strict exegesis. Clement accomplishes his purpose by the omission of "one" (μίαν); Tertullian, by a corresponding omission and a syntactical reconstruction. Yet, to call such liberty arbitrary is to misconstrue the good faith prompting these efforts. For we have in these examples par excellence instances of that "development of practical religious literature that raised no claim to stand on a level with the New Testament, but rather extracted from the New Testament the edifying teaching that it offered to the churches." [16] Thus, when the moralist urged a special point of view, he was forced at times to "extract" subtly, and sometimes desperately. For, as we have seen, the words of Jesus were his first and final authority in his appeal to the Christian community.

---

[14] "And none other, says the Lord, can make the hair white or black."

[15] "And do not swear by your head, for you cannot make one hair white or black."

[16] Harnack, p. 140.

Clement of Alexandria, *Quis Dives Salvetur* 37

καὶ μέλλων σπένδεσθαι καὶ λύτρον ἑαυτὸν ἐπιδιδοὺς καινὴν ἡμῖν διαθήκην
καταλιμπάνει· ἀγάπην ὑμῖν δίδωμι τὴν ἐμήν.[17]

John xiv.27

Εἰρήνην ἀφίημι ὑμῖν, εἰρήνην τὴν ἐμὴν δίδωμι ὑμῖν.[18]

Clement's emendation at this point is apparently in the
nature of a homiletic adaptation to context. The theme has
to do with the exaltation of God's love toward man as this
has been manifested by his sacrificial giving of himself
through his Son. Hence, "my love I give unto you" (ἀγάπην
ὑμῖν δίδωμι τὴν ἐμήν). Since, however, this passage is cited
with the purpose of prompting mankind (and especially, in
this instance, the rich man) to similar deeds of human kindness and of love, practical motives are obvious in the creation of this variant.

We shall observe within this category a group of variants
which turn about interests which one might call religious
and personal. Admittedly, religious and personal interests are
inextricably associated with each example set forth in this
monograph. It is, however, in order that we may witness
these motives in a somewhat heightened expression that the
following instances have been isolated.

Tertullian, *Adversus Marcionem* iv.17

Estote, inquit, misericordes, sicut pater vester miseratus est vestri.

Luke vi.36

Γίνεσθε οἰκτίρμονες καθὼς ὁ πατὴρ ὑμῶν οἰκτίρμων ἐστίν.[19]

---

[17] "And being about to be offered up and giving himself a ransom, he
left for us a new covenant — My love I give unto you."

[18] "Peace I leave with you; my peace I give to you."

[19] "Be merciful, even as your Father is merciful."

There is no attestation for Tertullian's "sicut pater vester miseratus est vestri." An examination of his context here is, however, instructive. Tertullian is deriding the ascription of the quality of love to a God other than the Creator. Of this "Other" Tertullian scoffs: "aut si alius nunc misericordiam praecepit, quia et ipse misericors sit, cur tanto aevo misericors mihi non fuit?" But since the fact of man's personal enjoyment of heaven-sent satisfactions is unequivocal, there follows the injunction to minister in kind; and surely the appended *vestri* has here the effect of personalizing the tone of the more generalized canonical injunction.

Apologia i.15

Γίνεσθε δὲ χρηστοὶ καὶ οἰκτίρμονες, ὡς καὶ ὁ πατὴρ ὑμῶν χρηστός ἐστι καὶ οἰκτίρμων.[20]

Stromata ii.19

γίνεσθε, φησὶν ὁ κύριος, ἐλεήμονες καὶ οἰκτίρμονες, ὡς ὁ πατὴρ ὑμῶν ὁ οὐράνιος οἰκτίρμων ἐστίν.[21]

Luke vi.36

Γίνεσθε οἰκτίρμονες καθὼς ὁ πατὴρ ὑμῶν οἰκτίρμων ἐστίν.

It may perhaps be conceded that χρηστός (kind) and ἐλεήμων (merciful) were added by Justin and by Clement for enhanced religious effect. Or it is possible to assert that we are concerned with phenomena easily accounted for on simple textual grounds. Thus the predicate χρηστός, used of God in Luke vi.35, was readily combined by Justin with vi.36 as indicated. Clement has apparently anticipated his quotation of Proverbs xxi.26, where the righteous man is represented as showing mercy and pity (ἐλεᾷ καὶ οἰκτίρει), and the added idea of mercy has been applied here also to God.

---

[20] "And be kind and merciful, as your Father also is kind and merciful."
[21] "Be merciful and compassionate, says the Lord, as your heavenly Father is compassionate."

Nevertheless, may not the readings represent equally the religious impulse issuing in expansive attribution to God, as well as an ethical and practical bent which enlarges the scope for man's emulation between which, perhaps, it is unnecessary to choose?

Irenaeus V.xxi.2

Scriptum est: Non in pane tantum vivit homo.

Paedagogus ii.1

οὐ γὰρ ἐπ' ἄρτῳ ζήσεται ὁ δίκαιος.[22]

Matthew iv. 4 (Luke iv.4)

Οὐκ ἐπ' ἄρτῳ μόνῳ ζήσεται ὁ ἄνθρωπος.[23]

With reference to the *vivit* of Irenaeus, it is perhaps improbable that we are dealing with the kind of concern for verbal detail manifested elsewhere (see p. 35, note). Nor, again, is the δίκαιος of Clement's intended merely to issue a warning against overindulgence (note context) especially to the "righteous man." It seems, rather, both in the insistence upon a present communion and in the reservation of this privilege for the righteous, that high devotional considerations are seriously to be reckoned with.[24]

Stromata vi.9

αἴτησαι, λέγων, καὶ ποιήσω· ἐννοήθητι καὶ δώσω.[25]

---

[22] "For the righteous man shall not live by bread."

[23] "Man shall not live by bread alone."

[24] It may be noted that these two quotations serve as excellent illustrations of the category of Contextual Adaptation previously suggested. According to the terms of both contexts, only so much of the text is indicated as is pertinent. In fact, so far as the efficacy of the "Word of God" is amply emphasized in the course of each discussion, it is highly probable that an intentionally abridged Matthean, as over against a Lucan, model was present the minds of the writers at this point.

[25] ". . . saying, Ask and I will do; think, and I will give."

Cf. Matthew vii.7

Αἰτεῖτε, καὶ δοθήσεται ὑμῖν.²⁶

Cf. Mark vi.22 (also Matthew vi.8; Ephesians iii.20)

Αἴτησόν με ὃ ἐὰν θέλῃς, καὶ δώσω σοι.²⁷

One is unable properly to speak of variation when the source of quotation is inconclusively established, although there are evident probable points of contact with the scriptural passages suggested. We have, nevertheless, what amounts to a fresh adaptation of the words of Jesus in Clement's probable quotation — an adaptation instinct with profound religious implications. Indeed, as to the man whose inner impulses are true and Godlike, as to the true Gnostic, God does not await his verbal petition (τούτου φωνὴν κατὰ τὴν εὐχὴν οὐκ ἀναμένει κύριος). This concept, at once a challenge to the ordinary Christian and an assurance to him who has thus attained, bespeaks a matrix which is less a practical motivation than an abiding religious faith.

Tertullian, *De Resurrectione Carnis* 34

*Feliciores enim, inquit, qui non vident et credent.*²⁷ᵃ

John xx.29

λέγει αὐτῷ [ὁ] Ἰησοῦς Ὅτι ἑώρακάς με πεπίστευκας; μακάριοι οἱ μὴ ἰδόντες καὶ πιστεύσασντες.²⁸

²⁶ "Ask and it will be given you."
²⁷ "Ask me for whatever you wish and I will grant it."
²⁷ᵃ It may, of course, be convincingly argued that the present tense, *vident*, represents merely a rendering of John's aorist participle. Even such a purely grammatical transcription, however, should not obscure Tertullian's emphasis upon the superior character of discipleship in his own day, as against a faith buttressed by more immediate evidence. Hence the possibility of an intentional verbal adjustment of the kind suggested on p. 53.
²⁸ "Jesus said to him, Have you believed because you have seen me? Blessed are those who have not seen and yet believe."

It is probable that there is represented in the tenses of *vident* and *credent* a kind of homiletic adaptation to circumstance. As might be supposed, in the light of the canonical reading, variant readings are available for these two verbs. The present readings, supported by A B C a and B C a, respectively, seem best supported intrinsically in view of the demands of Tertullian's argument. These variants, along with the comparative degree of the adjective, have their most plausible point of departure in urgently religious, as well as practical, premises.

There is within this order of emendations a series of remarkable readings growing out of what might be called exegetical or interpretive interests operative in the process of textual change. A typical illustration is afforded by various quotations of Luke xvi.10–12. They may be profitably considered as a group.

II Clement viii.5

λέγει γὰρ ὁ κύριος ἐν τῷ εὐαγγελίῳ· Εἰ τὸ μικρὸν οὐκ ἐτηρήσατε, τὸ μέγα τίς ὑμῖν δώσει; λέγω γὰρ ὑμῖν ὅτι ὁ πιστὸς ἐν ἐλαχίστῳ καὶ ἐν πολλῷ πιστός ἐστιν.[29]

Irenaeus II.xxxiv.3

Si in modico fideles non fuistis, quod magnum est quis dabit vobis?

Adversus Marcionem iv.33

Et si in alieno fideles inventi non estis, meum quis dabit vobis?

Luke xvi.10–12

ὁ πιστὸς ἐν ἐλαχίστῳ καὶ ἐν πολλῷ πιστός ἐστιν, καὶ ὁ ἐν ἐλαχίστῳ ἄδικος καὶ ἐν πολλῷ ἄδικός ἐστιν. εἰ οὖν ἐν τῷ ἀδίκῳ μαμωνᾷ πιστοὶ οὐκ

[29] "For the Lord says in the Gospel, If you did not keep [guard] that which is small, who shall give you that which is great? For I tell you that he who is faithful in that which is least, is faithful also in that which is much."

ἐγένεσθε, τὸ ἀληθινὸν τίς ὑμῖν πιστεύσει; καὶ εἰ ἐν τῷ ἀλλοτρίῳ πιστοὶ
οὐκ ἐγένεσθε, τὸ ἡμέτερον τίς δώσει ὑμῖν; [30]

It is to be noticed that in the text of Luke there is no
protasis and apodosis involving the antithesis "small" and
"great." II Clement, however, in his announced quotation
from "the Gospel" does present such a reading. It may, of
course, be argued that II Clement is probably quoting from
memory and that memory would quite easily have seized
upon such commonplace antonyms. Yet, these words do not
appear in Luke. More significantly, II Clement reproduces
exactly the preface to the saying (Luke xvi.10) involving
the considerably more difficult (mnemonically) "least"-
"much" contrast. All the more noticeable, therefore, is
Irenaeus' quotation in terms corresponding exactly to II
Clement's version, with the exception of the latter's ἐτηρήσατε
(kept). And this, it seems, may be satisfactorily accounted
for by II Clement's particular interest. For example, the
sense of the quotation, according to II Clement, "means this:
keep the flesh pure (τηρήσατε), and the seal of baptism un-
defiled." The term is therefore, quite probably, an interpolation at II Clement's own hand. Thus the confirmation furnished by the unusually consistent Irenaeus provokes the
conclusion that we are here probably in possession of a con-
structive oral summary of Luke xvi.10 available to these two
writers.

Equally difficult is the exegetical problem felt in the apodosis "who will give you that which is your own" (τὸ ὑμέτερον
τίς δώσει ὑμῖν). This reading, admitting of more ready apprehension on the part of, and in reference to, the Christian
community, is amply supported by ℵ A D Θ a f q.

---

[30] "He who is faithful in a very little is faithful also in much; and he who
is dishonest in a very little is dishonest also in much. If then you have not
been faithful in the unrighteous mammon, who will entrust to you the true
riches? And if you have not been faithful in that which is another's, who
will give you that which is our own?"

Tertullian's recording of what is intended to represent Marcion's reading reveals also an interpretive effort, presumably with dogmatic intent. For, according to Tertullian, the *meum* represents the interests of the Creator, who uncompromisingly imposes his righteous obligations upon mankind.

Stromata i.24

αἰτεῖσθε γάρ, φησί, τὰ μεγάλα, καὶ τὰ μικρὰ ὑμῖν προστεθήσεται.[31]

Matthew vi.33 (Luke xii.31)

ζητεῖτε δὲ πρῶτον τὴν βασιλείαν καὶ τὴν δικαιοσύνην αὐτοῦ, καὶ ταῦτα πάντα προστεθήσεται ὑμῖν.[32]

This quotation of Clement's is found also in the writings of Origen (three times) and of Eusebius. Resch records it as a *logion*.[33] But to label this an independent saying is, as always in such instances, to advance an assumption difficult to sustain. As in the case of Luke xvi.10–12 (though, obviously, with greater reservations), we should suggest that here also we probably have to do with a popular evangelic summary current in oral tradition — a summary, quite possibly of Matthew vi.33 (Luke xii.31), which must have figured prominently in Christian piety. On the other hand, to account for the verbatim continuance of this saying until the time of Eusebius, it is of course necessary to admit the probability of its crystallization in written form. Whatever Clement's source, however, it is reasonably clear that the words of Jesus have been thus graphically compressed to minister to the ethical and practical needs of the Christian community.

[31] "For, he says, Ask for what is great and the little things shall be yours as well."

[32] "But seek first the kingdom and his righteousness, and all these things shall be yours as well."

[33] *Agrapha*, *TU*, V, 4 (Leipzig, 1899), 114.

A necessary consideration within this category is that of a
set of variants due, it would seem, to certain circumstantial
exigencies. They reflect persecution and faction and in their
intent perform a kind of apologetic or hortatory function.

Justin Martyr, *Dialogus* 35.3

ἀναστήσονται πολλοὶ ψευδόχριστοι καὶ ψευδοαπόστολοι καὶ πολλοὺς τῶν
πιστῶν πλανήσουσιν.[34]

Matthew xxiv.11; Mark xiii.22

καὶ πολλοὶ ψευδοπροφῆται ἐγερθήσονται καὶ πλανήσουσιν πολλούς . . .
ἐγερθήσονται γὰρ ψευδόχριστοι καὶ ψευδοπροφῆται.[35]

In response to Trypho's jibe that even so-called Christians
eat idol sacrifices, Justin advances the explanation here recorded. Christ had foreseen, therefore, the folly of those so
misled, including "many of the faithful" (τῶν πιστῶν) — an
interpolation of high apologetic importance in the scheme of
Justin's defense.

Tertullian, *De Fuga in Persecutione* 7

Felices qui persecutionem passi fuerint causa nominis mei.

Matthew v.11

μακάριοί ἐστε ὅταν ὀνειδίσωσιν ὑμᾶς καὶ διώξωσιν καὶ εἴπωσιν πᾶν
πονηρὸν καθ' ὑμῶν ψευδόμενοι ἕνεκεν ἐμοῦ.[36]

Tertullian offers this quotation in support of other sentiment intended to inspire firmness in the face of persecution.
And, though he seems to present but a rough paraphrase of

---

[34] "And many false Christs and false apostles will arise, and will deceive
many of the faithful."

[35] "And many false prophets will arise and lead many astray." "For false
Christs and false prophets will arise . . ."

[36] "Blessed are you when men revile you and persecute you and utter all
kinds of evil against you falsely on my account."

his Matthean model, the *causa nominis mei* introduces a significant point of interest. The fact that Christians had been indicted by the Roman government simply for the name Christian (*crimen nominis*) had been bitterly deplored by Tertullian.[37] It is perhaps no accident, therefore, that persecution "for my sake" here becomes persecution "for my name's sake," with the promise of heavenly blessing.[38]

[37] R. E. Roberts, *The Theology of Tertullian*, estimates the date of the *Apologeticus* to have been about 197; that of *De fuga* about 212.

[38] This is not to suggest, of course, that the present reading of Tertullian implies a second-century date for διὰ τὸ ὄνομά μου (Mt. x.22 and parallels). Yet, though it is probably improper here to speak of Tertullian's "harmonization" of the present text with Mt. x.22 (cf. pp. 24ff.), practical circumstances may well have made for the crystallized association of these two texts in a manner which would seem to render superfluous the appeal to deliberate literary refinement.

VIII

Dogmatic Motivation

Consistent with the attitude which induced to free adaptation of Scripture for ethical and practical ends was the spirit which made for enlargement or suppression of textual details in the interest of dogma. The sphere of this dogmatic activity was, however (with outstanding and obvious exceptions), a circumscribed one. For we are dealing, for the most part, with the efforts of men who themselves "abode in the teaching of Christ" and who sought thus earnestly to strengthen their brothers. Yet dogmatic preoccupation, like ethical concern, was an equally inevitable expression of a "practical religious literature" ministering to readers at various levels of culture. Independent investigations previously noted (pp. 6–7, note 12) reveal, to be sure, but meagre signs of dogmatic activity. The following demonstration on strictly patristic grounds seems to imply, however, a more vigorous dogmatic interest in the text of the New Testament than our present data would permit us to detect.

I Clement xlvi.7–8

μνήσθητε τῶν λόγων τοῦ κυρίου Ἰησοῦ. εἶπεν γάρ· Οὐαὶ τῷ ἀνθρώπῳ ἐκείνῳ· καλὸν ἦν αὐτῷ εἰ οὐκ ἐγεννήθη, ἢ ἕνα τῶν ἐκλεκτῶν μου σκανδαλίσαι· κρεῖττον ἦν αὐτῷ περιτεθῆναι μύλον καὶ καταποντισθῆναι εἰς τὴν θάλασσαν, ἢ ἕνα τῶν ἐκλεκτῶν μου διαστρέψαι.[1] (Cf. *Strom.* iii.18.)

---

[1] "Remember the words of the Lord Jesus, for he said: Woe unto that man: it would have been better for him if he had not been born, than that he should offend one of my elect; it would be better for him that a millstone

Matthew xxvi.24 (Mark xiv.21)

οὐαὶ δὲ τῷ ἀνθρώπῳ ἐκείνῳ δι' οὗ ὁ υἱὸς τοῦ ἀνθρώπου παραδίδοται· καλὸν
ἦν αὐτῷ εἰ οὐκ ἐγεννήθη ὁ ἄνθρωπος ἐκεῖνος.[2]

Matthew xviii.6–7

ὃς δ' ἂν σκανδαλίσῃ ἕνα τῶν μικρῶν τούτων τῶν πιστευόντων εἰς ἐμέ,
συμφέρει αὐτῷ ἵνα κρεμασθῇ μύλος ὀνικὸς περὶ τὸν τράχηλον αὐτοῦ καὶ
καταποντισθῇ ἐν τῷ πελάγει τῆς θαλάσσης . . . οὐαὶ . . . δι' οὗ τὸ
σκάνδαλον ἔρχεται.[3]

Various authorities account for Clement's composite reproduction on the basis of his probable use of some kind of cate-
chetical source, of oral tradition, or simply as a quotation
made from memory. Despite the plausibility of the first two
conjectures, the suggestion of mnemonic citation seems
here most applicable. This selection of verses might, indeed,
have existed in documentary form, but the ideas are also
easily associated and so probably constitute a *memoriter*
appeal to canonical sources.

One is here impressed with Clement's use of ἐκλεκτῶν
(elect) for μικρῶν (little ones). A quotation from Clement
of Alexandria in a form almost identical with that of Clement of Rome — including also ἐκλεκτῶν — proves little.
Clement of Alexandria's use of I Clement has been reasonably well established. In spite of the possible aberrations at-
tending mnemonic quotation, it seems defensible to accept
ἐκλεκτῶν as having been deliberately employed. For the aim
of Clement at this point, and elsewhere throughout the epis-

---

should be hung on him, and he be cast into the sea, than that he should
turn aside one of my elect."

[2] "Woe to that man by whom the Son of Man is betrayed! It would
have been better for that man if he had not been born."

[3] "But whoever causes one of these little ones who believe in me to sin,
it would be better for him to have a great millstone fastened round his neck
and to drown in the depth of the sea. . . Woe to the man by whom the
temptation [to sin] comes!"

tle, is to vindicate the sacred and divinely ordered office of
the bishop and of the other spiritually selected officials. These
persons, Clement contends, "God has chosen (ἐκλέλεκται)
for his priesthood and ministry" (xliii). Hence the condem-
nation incurred by those who offend. To say, then, that it
was Clement's intention thus to glorify the youthful hierarchy
of office is to state what is easily conceded. It is also possible
to detect here an intentionally conceived variant in dogmatic
support of this end.

Didache i.2

πρῶτον ἀγαπήσεις τὸν θεὸν τὸν ποιήσαντά σε, δεύτερον τὸν πλησίον
σου ὡς σεαυτόν.[4]

Justin Martyr, *Apologia* i.16.6

κύριον τὸν θεόν σου προσκυνήσεις καὶ αὐτῷ μόνῳ λατρεύσεις ἐξ ὅλης τῆς
καρδίας σου καὶ ἐξ ὅλης τῆς ἰσχύος σου, κύριον τὸν θεὸν τὸν ποιήσαντά σε.[5]

Apologia i.16.7

οὐδεὶς ἀγαθὸς εἰ μὴ ὁ θεὸς ὁ ποιήσας πάντα.[6]

Luke x.27; Mark xii.31

ἀγαπήσεις κύριον τὸν θεόν σου ἐξ ὅλης καρδίας σου καὶ ἐν ὅλῃ τῇ ψυχῇ
σου καὶ ἐν ὅλῃ τῇ ἰσχύι σου καὶ ἐν ὅλῃ τῇ διανοίᾳ σου . . . δευτέρα
αὕτη Ἀγαπήσεις τὸν πλησίον σου ὡς σεαυτόν.[7]

Mark x.18

οὐδεὶς ἀγαθὸς εἰ μὴ εἷς ὁ θεός.[8]

[4] "First, you shall love God, who made you; secondly, your neighbor as
yourself."
[5] "You shall worship the Lord your God, and him only shall you serve,
with all your heart, and with all your strength, the Lord God that made you."
[6] "No one is good but God, who made all things."
[7] "You shall love the Lord your God with all you heart, and with all
your soul, and with all your strength, and with all your mind . . . The second
is this, You shall love your neighbor as yourself."
[8] "No one is good but God alone."

Noticeable in these quotations is what seems to be an extraneous interest in the creative activity of God. Appended to the abbreviated "summary of the Law" reproduced in the *Didache*, the τὸν ποιήσαντά σε (who made you) is probably in this setting to be ascribed to oral tradition, presumably of Jewish origin. Justin's free quotation involving the identical phrase is due probably to the same or to a similar source. His repetition of this idea in a different connection, nevertheless, suggests a rather fluid application more compatible with an oral than with a stereotyped documentary version. This, of course, cannot be urged. In neither of Justin's contexts, however, is the idea demanded in a manner suggestive of its being an independent creation. Thus the essential Jewishness of the sentiment here indicated leads one to suspect that Justin, along with the *Didache*, is reproducing from an uncanonical source a sentiment of prior urgency in the sphere of Jewish dogmatics.

Apologia i.15

Εἰ ἀγαπᾶτε τοὺς ἀγαπῶντας ὑμᾶς, τί καινὸν ποιεῖτε; καὶ γὰρ οἱ πόρνοι τοῦτο ποιοῦσιν.[9]

Matthew v.46 (Luke vi.32)

ἐὰν γὰρ ἀγαπήσητε τοὺς ἀγαπῶντας ὑμᾶς, τίνα μισθὸν ἔχετε; οὐχὶ καὶ οἱ τελῶναι τὸ αὐτὸ ποιοῦσιν;[10]

Justin's τί καινὸν ποιεῖτε (what new thing do you do) is a significant expression of the emergent self-consciousness of the early Christian community as representing in history a peculiar, indeed, a "new" people. Harnack asserts: "But for Christians who knew they were the old and the new People,

[9] "If you love those that love you, what new thing do you do? For even fornicators do this."

[10] "For if you love those who love you, what reward have you; do not even the tax collectors do the same?"

it was not enough to set this self-consciousness over against the Jews alone, or to contend with them for the possession of the promises and of the sacred book; settled on the soil of the Greek and Roman empire, they had to define their position." [11]

In the realm of Christian ethics Justin, in virtue of his adaptation, is seen thus to contribute to this extensive process of "definition" observable in the literature of the second century.

Clement of Alexandria, *Stromata* iii.6

ἦλθεν ὁ υἱὸς τοῦ ἀνθρώπου ἐσθίων καὶ πίνων, καὶ λέγουσιν· ἰδοὺ ἄνθρωπος φάγος καὶ οἰνοπότης, φίλος τελωνῶν καὶ ἁμαρτωλός.[12]

Matthew xi.19 (Luke vii.33–34)

ἦλθεν ὁ υἱὸς τοῦ ἀνθρώπου ἐσθίων καὶ πίνων, καὶ λέγουσιν Ἰδοὺ ἄνθρωπος φάγος καὶ οἰνοπότης, τελωνῶν φίλος καὶ ἁμαρτωλῶν.[13]

ἁμαρτωλός (sinner) in Clement's quotation, as Barnard points out, marks the only instance of the nominative case in this connection. Clement again quotes this verse (*Paedagogus* ii.2) but omits καὶ ἁμαρτωλός. Apparently, however, there was known to Clement a reading involving the word "sinner." Certainly it is difficult to conceive how Clement, quoting even from memory (which assumption this quotation does not justify), could have originated the reading. Perhaps, indeed, his omission of the phrase elsewhere might argue for conscious aversion. It is nevertheless significant that such a reading has not survived in any other extant source. It is more interesting still that it has been preserved at all.

[11] *The Expansion of Christianity*, trans. James Moffatt (2 vols.; New York, 1904), I, 303f.
[12] "The Son of Man came eating and drinking, and they say, Behold, a glutton and a drunkard, a friend of tax collectors and a sinner."
[13] "The Son of Man came eating and drinking, and they say, Behold, a glutton and a drunkard, a friend of tax collectors and sinners."

Apologia i.63

Οὐδεὶς ἔγνω τὸν πατέρα εἰ μὴ ὁ υἱός, οὐδὲ τὸν υἱὸν εἰ μὴ ὁ πατὴρ καὶ οἷς ἂν ὁ υἱὸς ἀποκαλύψῃ.[14]

Matthew xi.27 (Luke x.22)

οὐδεὶς ἐπιγινώσκει τὸν υἱὸν εἰ μὴ ὁ πατήρ, οὐδὲ τὸν πατέρα τις ἐπιγινώσκει εἰ μὴ ὁ υἱὸς καὶ ᾧ ἐὰν βούληται ὁ υἱὸς ἀποκαλύψαι.[15]

Justin three times quotes this passage and each time with the inversion noted. An almost exclusive preference for this order may be documented, too, from the writings of Clement of Alexandria, Irenaeus, and Tertullian.[16] The clear inference from this fact Barnard draws in these words: "Either . . . the Fathers were curiously consistent in their misquotation of this verse, or else there was a type of text fairly widely current from the second to the fourth century which is not represented in the MSS and versions now extant." [17]

Such "consistent" misquotation would obviously be difficult to account for without appeal to some kind of documentary authority — although it is rather the reason for the accomplished fact which is perhaps of greater importance here. It is probable, therefore, that this phenomenon suggests less a view of philosophic transcendence and unknowability with reference to God than of the mediacy and the immediacy of Christ with reference to the believer. Irenaeus, therefore, says of Christ in terms representative of these writers and in tones suggestive of creedal declaration: "vere homo et vere Deus . . . Omnia autem Filius administrans Patri, perfecit

---

[14] "No one knows the Father except the Son; nor the Son, except the Father, and they to whom the Son reveals him."

[15] "No one knows the Son except the Father, and no one knows the Father except the Son, and any one to whom the Son chooses to reveal him."

[16] *Strom.* vii.18, II.xiv.7, *Adv. Marc.* ii.27, respectively, in addition to several other occurrences in these writers.

[17] Barnard, p. 16.

ab initio usque ad finem et sine illo nemo potest cognoscere
Deum" [18] — a dogmatic formulation whose roots have been
nurtured by highly sensitive religious perceptions.

Stromata vi.7

μὴ εἴπητε ἑαυτοῖς διδάσκαλον ἐπὶ τῆς γῆς.[19]

Matthew xxiii.8–9

ὑμεῖς δὲ μὴ κληθῆτε ῾Ραββεί, εἷς γάρ ἐστιν ὑμῶν ὁ διδάσκαλος . . . καὶ
πατέρα μὴ καλέσητε ὑμῶν ἐπὶ τῆς γῆς.[20]

"Remarkable" indeed is Clement's combination of Matthew xxiii.8,9 — a reading which Clement employs elsewhere
(*Stromata* ii.4). Origen (*Homilia in Jeremiam* x) likewise
uses this combined text. Clement reveals further an interesting correspondence with D and certain Latin versions which
read here ὑμῖν (ἑαυτοῖς).

---

[18] IV.vi.7. On textual grounds, however, Professor Harnack offers a series
of stimulating conjectures with reference to this verse. He thinks, for example, γινώσκει to have arisen in Luke (and so in Matthew from Luke) as
a result of Irenaeus' criticism (IV.1) of the reading ἔγνω as a heretical
forgery. Harnack's demonstration from numerous Christian sources, however,
shows ἔγνω to have had wide currency. Arguing from the supposition that
ἔγνω represents an original Lucan reading for this text, Harnack continues:
"The historic aorist ἔγνω suits excellently the Son's knowledge of the Father,
but it does not suit so well the Father's knowledge of the Son; this has
been noticed by thoughtful copyists, who have tried to overcome the difficulty . . . In Codex Vercell. of St. Luke we even now read the saying without the clause concerning 'knowledge of the Son' . . . The clause καὶ ᾧ ἂν
ὁ υἱὸς ἀποκαλύψῃ suits only the clause οὐδεὶς ἔγνω τίς ἐστιν ὁ πατὴρ εἰ μὴ
ὁ υἱός, but not the other clause with which it is connected above in St. Luke
(the Son is God's interpreter and not his own). This also has been correctly
seen by the copyists, who have accordingly overcome the difficulty by trans-
position . . . In my opinion, we are simply forced to the conclusion that in
St. Luke the words καὶ τίς ἐστιν ὁ υἱὸς εἰ μὴ ὁ πατήρ were wanting" (*The
Sayings of Jesus*, trans. J. R. Wilkinson, New York, 1908, pp. 281–293).
[19] "Do not call them [men] teacher on earth."
[20] "But you are not to be called rabbi, for you have one teacher. And
call no man your father on earth."

Apparently the interest thus manifested is in the nature of a dogmatic confirmation of Christ's role as the eternal instructor of mankind. More specifically, continues Clement: "He is called wisdom by all the prophets; this is he who is teacher [διδάσκαλος] of all that has come into being, the fellow-counsellor with God. . ."

Irenaeus IV.xxiv.2

Ne putetis quoniam veni dissolvere legem aut prophetas: non enim veni dissolvere sed adimplere. Amen dico vobis: Donec pertranseat caelum et terra, iota unum aut unus apex non transiet a lege et prophetis, quoadusque omnia fiant.

Matthew v.17

Μὴ νομίσητε ὅτι ἦλθον καταλῦσαι τὸν νόμον ἢ τοὺς προφήτας· οὐκ ἦλθον καταλῦσαι ἀλλὰ πληρῶσαι· ἀμὴν γὰρ λέγω ὑμῖν, ἕως ἂν παρέλθῃ ὁ οὐρανὸς καὶ ἡ γῆ, ἰῶτα ἓν ἢ μία κερέα οὐ μὴ παρέλθῃ ἀπὸ τοῦ νόμου ἕως [ἂν] πάντα γένηται.[21]

The Old Testament constituted, of course, a primary source of evidence for the Christian community. Its pronouncements served both as shield against heretics and as surety for believers. With such a dual purpose Irenaeus engages Matthew v.17 as he seeks, on biblical grounds, to validate the coming of Christ by means of an elaborate argument from prophecy. Pointed, therefore, is his insertion of *prophetis*, an earnest now of equal importance with the Law as to the fulfillment of God's announced purposes.[22]

---

[21] "Think not that I have come to abolish the law and the prophets; I have come not to abolish them but to fulfill them. For truly, I say to you, till heaven and earth pass away, not an iota, not a dot, will pass from the law until all is accomplished."

[22] It may, of course, be urged that the "addition of 'and prophets' could also be simply adjusting to earlier formula." Irenaeus' argument, however, seems to demand a conscious adaptation of the kind here assumed.

Irenaeus III.xvi.5

Oportet enim, inquit, Filium hominis multa pati et reprobari et crucifigi et die tertio resurgere.

Luke ix.22 (Mark viii.31)

εἰπὼν ὅτι Δεῖ τὸν υἱὸν τοῦ ἀνθρώπου πολλὰ παθεῖν καὶ ἀποδοκιμασθῆναι ἀπὸ τῶν πρεσβυτέρων καὶ ἀρχιερέων καὶ γραμματέων καὶ ἀποκτανθῆναι καὶ τῇ τρίτῃ ἡμέρᾳ ἐγερθῆναι.[23]

It appears significant that Irenaeus both here and elsewhere (III.xviii.4) presents *crucifigi* for ἀποκτανθῆναι (killed). It is perhaps possible that the quotation thus denuded of "scribes, Pharisees, and chief priests" (*sacerdotibus* appears in III.xviii.4) reflects already the influence of some kind of creedal formulation.[24] Whether, therefore, *crucifigi* is to be ascribed to such a recollection on the part of Irenaeus or is rather the influence of the actual course of events is not certain.[25] Since, however, both contexts emphasize the large importance of Jesus' predictive insight, he being the Christ, the presumption is attractive which sees in this emendation an attempt to suggest a Messianic anticipation of detail worthy of the office.

Tertullian, *De Baptismo* 12

Qui semel lavit, non habet necesse rursum.

[23] ". . . saying, The Son of Man must suffer many things, and be rejected by the elders and chief priests and scribes, and be killed, and on the third day be raised."

[24] Cf. Tertullian, *Adv. Marc.* iv.43.

[25] Among other possibilities, certainly Mt. xx.19 and Lk. xxiv.7 should be cited as plausible models for *crucifigi*. It may be asked, too, whether discrepancies of quotation may not be accounted for simply on the basis of unconscious harmonization. As elsewhere with Irenaeus, however, this does not appear to be an instance of careless quotation.

John xiii.10

Ὁ λελουμένος οὐκ ἔχει χρείαν [εἰ μὴ τοὺς πόδας] νίψασθαι.[26]

Noteworthy is Tertullian's appropriation of John xiii.10 to apply as a dogmatic injunction to a unique participation in the baptismal rite. His emphasis upon a single performance of the ceremony, however, is not to be confused with the problem of heretical baptism which was soon to become acute. Tertullian strongly disavows the efficacy of any such heretical activity.

The signification of the purported dictum, supported by an appeal to Ephesians iv.5 (cf. also Hebrews vi.4), the moralist sets forth in the following terms (chapter 15): "semel ergo lavacrum inimus, semel delicta diluuntur, quia ea iterari non oportet."

Tertullian, *De Resurrectione Carnis* 61

Non in pane vivit homo, sed in dei verbo.[27]

Matthew iv.4 (Luke iv.4)

Γέγραπται Οὐκ ἐπ᾽ ἄρτῳ μόνῳ ζήσεται ὁ ἄνθρωπος, ἀλλ᾽ ἐπὶ παντὶ ῥήματι ἐκπορευομένῳ διὰ στόματος θεοῦ.[28]

Tertullian's omission of reference to "mouth" in connection with God (ἐκπορευομένῳ διὰ στόματος) is supported by D b g k (k omitting also θεοῦ). This is an instance less of a Western noninterpolation, so-called, in view of the reading of Deuteronomy viii.3, than of what appears to be studied omission. To see in the quotation an attempt thus to avoid the crude anthropomorphism involved in the original text seems readily to account for the change.

---

[26] "He who has bathed does not need to wash, except for his feet."
[27] MSS c d read *vivet*.
[28] "It is written, Man shall not live by bread alone, but by every word that proceeds from the mouth of God."

ADDITIONAL NOTE ON DOGMATIC MOTIVATION

Tertullian, *De Oratione* 4

Fiat voluntas tua in caelis et in terra.

Matthew vi.10

γενηθήτω τὸ θέλημά σου, ὡς ἐν οὐρανῷ καὶ ἐπὶ γῆς.[29]

Along with Tertullian, D* a b c k omit the comparative adverb ὡς (as) in this clause from the Lord's Prayer.
F. H. Chase calls attention to passages whose structure and
thought bear close resemblance to the Western and Neutral
readings represented above in quotation and model.[30] The
two following examples are typical of his selections: Psalm
cxxxiv.6 ("Everything whatsoever the Lord wished he did
both in heaven and [καὶ] in earth"); and I Maccabees iii.60
(". . . as [ὡς]may be the will in heaven, so shall he do").
It is therefore apparent from these and other examples that
the concept "earth and heaven," representing areas of God's
impartial activity (ὡς and καί apparently being used inter-
changeably in this connection), was not a rare one in Jewish
religious thought. It is thus perhaps unnecessary to speak of
"motivated" variation since we are quite probably dealing,
in these two versions, with independent creations; and,
again, with ideas readily reconciled from a Jewish point of
view.

[29] "Thy kingdom come, thy will be done on earth as it is in heaven."
[30] *The Lord's Prayer in the Early Church, Texts and Studies*, I, 3 (Cambridge, England, 1891), 40f.

IX

Heretical Adaptation

We have noted that the examples treated above as "dogmatic" were consistently in the nature of emendations subsidiary to the tenets of orthodoxy. In striking contrast, however, are certain instances of heterodox activity reported also by the writers dealt with. In quoting a heretic the Christian writer of course felt bound to observe no strict canons of accuracy. Since, indeed, such quotations were made with a view toward refutation, one may wonder just how trustworthy these representations have been. It is thus our purpose, in the light of these limitations, to observe rather the spirit of the changes thus alleged in the interest of special dogmatic predilections. An attempt will be made merely to identify, not to discuss, the heresy involved, with the intention of illustrating characteristic phases of Docetic and Gnostic beliefs.

Irenaeus I.viii.2 (John xii.27)

Et quid dicam nescio.

The appended *nescio* is said to have been added by the Valentinians in the interest of their heresy. This is plausible since Hachamoth, to whom the words are ascribed, representing the passion of σωφία (Wisdom), is thought to be possessed of all material imperfections. Such blemishes, the inheritance of a brute creation, are the irreconcilable obstacles to redemptive knowledge.

Irenaeus I.xx.2 (Matthew xi.28–29)

Venite ad me omnes qui laboratis et onerati estis et discite a me.

Irenaeus offers this abbreviated quotation of Matthew
xi.28–29 as a primary source of authority for the Ptolemaic
Gnostics (and for one Mark in particular) in reference to
the hidden wisdom to be obtained exclusively from their
peculiar enlightenment.

Clement of Alexandria, *Stromata* iv.6 (Matthew v.10)

ὥς τινες τῶν μετατιθέντων τὰ εὐαγγέλια· μακάριοι, φησίν, οἱ δεδιωγμένοι
ὑπὲρ τῆς δικαιοσύνης, ὅτι αὐτοὶ ἔσονται τέλειοι.[1]

This reference by Clement of Alexandria is presumably to
the Carpocrations, of whose beliefs and practices he has just
concluded a violent refutation (*Stromata* iii). The "perfect"
state of the "elect," according to their persuasion, is the
more conspicuously evidenced by conditions however degenerate, morally or socially, either in which they may indulge
or to which they may be subject.

Hippolytus, *Refutatio Omnium Haeresium* v.26 (John xix.26)

ὁ δὲ καταλιπὼν τὸ σῶμα τῆς Ἐδὲμ πρὸς τὸ ξύλον, ἀνέβη πρὸς τὸν
ἀγαθόν· εἰπὼν δὲ τῇ Ἐδέμ· γύναι, ἀπέχεις σου τὸν υἱόν, τουτέστι τὸν
ψυχικὸν ἄνθρωπον.[2]

According to Naassene apprehension, the Divine Spirit
(here, Baruch) did not suffer or die on the cross. For there
was left only the bodily remains of Jesus to Edem (Israel),
his persecutor and the spouse of Elohim; the spirit of Jesus,
too, ascending to ὁ ἀγαθός (the Good One).

---

[1] "As certain of those who alter the gospels say, Blessed are they that
are persecuted for righteousness' sake, for they shall be perfect."

[2] "But he, leaving the body of Edem on the cross [the tree], ascended to
the Good One, Edem saying to the woman, You have received your son,
that is, the earthly man."

The Gospel According to Peter v (Mark xv.34; Matthew xxvii.46)

καὶ ὁ κύριος ἀνεβόησε λέγων Ἡ δύναμίς μου, ἡ δύναμις, κατέλειψάς με· [3]

The assumption is here entertained, on the basis of Dr. Swete's discussion of the problems involved,[4] that the Akhmîm fragment presents features which may be reasonably identified with Docetic interests. Along with other indications, ἡ δύναμις (the Power from above), instead of ὁ θεός (θεέ, God), may be cited as a point of rather definite contact with that school of thought concerned with the distinction between the Impassible Christ and the natural body which was, or appeared to be, his earthly habitation.

On the other hand, there remains the possibility that Semitic influence might be seen to account for the reading *dunamis*. Genesis (xxxi.29), Proverbs (iii.27), Micah (ii.1) employ *el* in the sense of "power." In patristic literature Justin Martyr (*Dialogus* 125) first makes the association of the Hebrew *el* with the Greek *dunamis*. Eusebius (*Demonstratio Evangelica* X.viii.30) approves Aquila's rendering of the Matthean *eli* (xxvii.46) as "my strength." The Hebrew root for "God" and for "power" being in both instances *el*, therefore, it is conceivable that some such association might here have been made; in which case it would be unnecessary to allege Docetic affinity, at least at this point.

[3] "And the Lord cried out saying, "My power, my power, you have left me."

[4] *The Gospel of Peter* (London, 1893), *passim*.

PART TWO

Antilegomena

X

Agrapha

By way of comparison with the treatment given the New Testament text by men quoting purposely from canonical sources, it would seem well to examine some characteristic second-century dominical utterances whose provenance, despite the ascription, is not so clearly discerned. Such expressions have been discussed under the heading "Agrapha," the assumption being that "these sayings are stray survivals from an unwritten tradition, orally preserved and running parallel with the written Gospels." It will be seen, however, upon the application of certain obvious critical criteria, that few sayings remain concerning which a presumption for genuineness can be safely maintained. To be sure, the role of subjective judgment is a large one in the process of selection. It is easy to see, too, how many so-called *agrapha* may have had their origin in the opinion of modern scholarship. For example, it is highly doubtful that Justin Martyr intended to present the following quotation as representing, in its entirety, an independent saying of Jesus.

Apologia i.15

εἶπε δὲ οὕτως· Οὐκ ἦλθον καλέσαι δικαίους ἀλλ' ἁμαρτωλοὺς εἰς μετάνοιαν· θέλει γὰρ ὁ πατὴρ ὁ οὐράνιος τὴν μετάνοιαν τοῦ ἁμαρτωλοῦ, ἢ τὴν κόλασιν αὐτοῦ.[1]

---

[1] "He spoke thus: I come not to call the righeous, but sinners to repentance. For the heavenly Father desires rather the repentance than the punishment of the sinner."

The first part of this citation has its model in Mark ii.17 (and parallels). The complement seems clearly in the nature of an explanation, the sentiment of which might be readily documented from Ezekiel (xxxiii.11); or, if their currency be granted, from II Peter (iii.9) and I Timothy (ii.4), which are themselves indebted, quite possibly, to the Old Testament. It would be, therefore, precarious to insist, as does Resch, "dass der in Rede stehende Zusatz zu dem Citat gehöre und auf einem Herrenwort ruhe." [2] In addition to erroneous and careless ascription to Jesus of biblical sentiment, patristic homiletic paraphrase and, occasionally, common errors of transcription [3] have swelled the list of "half-strange" sayings purporting to supplement our canonical collection. For the most part, nevertheless, it will be apparent that our four Gospels have been used merely in varying combinations in the formulation of pronouncements considered "helpful" to the reader. There are, further, instances wherein the authority of Jesus has been boldly enlisted to sponsor a body of sentiment wholly alien to orthodox tradition. Such, indeed, is the case with certain Jewish-Christian gospels with which we shall have occasion to deal. In either setting, the words of Jesus, recast or invented, were thus "designed to serve the interests of faith in its controversy with various forms of unbelief, or to answer the special needs of some Christian community which looked at the evangelic tradition from its own angle and saw in Christ what others had not seen; and the peculiarities which they exhibited indicated wherein the earlier writings had proved unsatisfactory. Thus many Gospels arose, each in its own way reflecting the reli-

---

[2] *Agrapha*, p. 252.

[3] Professor Ropes calls attention to a Latin reading for *Epistola Barnabae*, iv.9: "Sicut dicit filius Dei, Resistamus omni iniquitati et odio habeamus eam," which is an obviously degenerate form of what appears to be the original Greek, ὡς πρέπει [*sicut decet*] κτλ.

gious interests of its readers and the conceptions which they had formed of the person and ministry of Christ." [4]

It is, of course, difficult to speak of motivation in attempting to interpret the intent of most "sayings." Their transmission without context and the fragmentary remains of these gospels make for uncertain conjecture, by and large. Nor, as we have seen, does patristic employment of such fragments point infallibly to the sentiment they conveyed in their original settings. Yet, wherever variation from canonical sources can be detected, an effort will be made to identify the nature of the change involved. This would entail necessarily a more or less complete analysis of the several *agrapha* and fragments in the establishing of their probable origins. Without our losing sight of the essential purpose of this study, however, a few *agrapha* have been considered which have no obvious point of contact with the canonical text. These have been included to give an insight into the kind of supposed sayings of Jesus which the Fathers saw fit to preserve because of their intrinsic importance for the Christian community. Discussion of variants throughout Part II will be more conveniently given according to source rather than category as in Part I.

I Clement xiii.2–3

οὕτως γὰρ εἶπεν· Ἐλεᾶτε ἵνα ἐλεηθῆτε· ἀφίετε ἵνα ἀφεθῇ ὑμῖν· ὡς ποιεῖτε, οὕτως ποιηθήσεται ὑμῖν· ὡς δίδοτε, οὕτως δοθήσεται ὑμῖν· ὡς κρίνετε, οὕτως κριθήσεσθε· ὡς χρηστεύεσθε, οὕτως χρηστευθήσεται ὑμῖν· ᾧ μέτρῳ μετρεῖτε, ἐν αὐτῷ μετρηθήσεται ὑμῖν.[5]

---

[4] A. F. Findlay, *Byways in Early Christian Literature* (Edinburgh, 1923), p. 28.

[5] "He spoke thus: Be merciful that you may obtain mercy. Forgive that you may be forgiven. As you do, so shall it be done unto you. As you give, so shall it be given unto you. As you judge, so shall you be judged. As you are kind, so shall kindness be shown you. The measure you give shall be the measure you get back."

This passage from Clement has been minutely examined
by the Committee of the Oxford Society of Historical Theology. The points of difference and similarity with reference
to both Matthew and Luke have been carefully set forth.
The committee cite Polycarp, the *Didascalia*, and Macarius
as sources for a similar, but not identical, reproduction of
these verses. They "incline to think that we have in Clement
of Rome a citation from some written or unwritten form of
'Catechesis' as to our Lord's teaching current in the Roman
church." [6] Professor Ropes is of the opinion that we have to
do with a recension of canonical material (Luke vi.36–38),
but that the phenomenon, on still another view, lends strong
support to the theory of a pre-canonical gospel.[7] It seems
significant "that the series of phrases as it is found in Polycarp and the *Didascalia* is incomplete, and not in the same
order as in Clement of Rome." For if this observation indicates the absence of a common documentary source for these
writers, may it not also suggest an oral version of these
teachings with which they were acquainted? Such an oral
compendium of the gospel ethic could readily account for
the variations here evident.[8] Under such circumstances, of
course, one would be impressed in these verses less by "motivated" variation than by the strict legalistic commitment to
the "way of life" which their sentiments suggest.

Didache i.2

πάντα δὲ ὅσα ἐὰν θελήσῃς μὴ γίνεσθαί σοι, καὶ σὺ ἄλλῳ μὴ ποίει.[9]

The *Didache* is mentioned as the earliest Christian document incorporating this so-called negative version of the

---

[6] *The New Testament in the Apostolic Fathers* (Oxford, 1905), p. 61.

[7] *Die Sprüche Jesu, TU*, XIV, 2 (Leipzig, 1896), 15.

[8] Harnack and colleagues and Bishop Lightfoot think that the discrepancies of quotation here may be satisfactorily accounted for on the assumption that Clement was quoting canonical material from memory.

[9] "And whatsoever you would not have done to yourself, do not to another."

Golden Rule. This negative form (not verbatim) appears also, presumably very early, in Codex D and in eleven cursives by way of appendage to Acts xv.20, 29. Tobit and Philo constitute still earlier Jewish witnesses for the negative saying (variously recorded), which is attributed by Jews to Rabbi Hillel. Rendel Harris cites the following Jewish commentary on *Pirke Aboth*: "The commandment for the 'love of the brotherhood' is one of the commandments based upon the law and is to be interpreted thereby; as it is said, 'Thou shalt love they neighbor as thyself' (Leviticus xix.18), and all men are bound by it. Hillel the elder interpreted this saying and said, 'What to thyself is hateful, do not to thy neighbor.' " [10]

The positive adaptation of this sentiment, therefore (Luke vi.31; Matthew vii.12), scarcely admits of comparison with its apparent Jewish prototype as "better" or "worse." The occurrence affords rather an instructive example of the harmony existing between rabbinic and Christian traditions in some of their more fundamental expressions. A few modern commentators, however, see in the negative rendering an inferior (*minderwertige*) formulation of the sentiment. This seems to suggest the ethical and religious motivation prompting "improvement" through positive emendation at the hand of some Christian scribe.

Didache xvi.4, 6a

αὐξανούσης γὰρ τῆς ἀνομίας μισήσουσιν ἀλλήλους καὶ διώξουσι καὶ παραδώσουσι, καὶ τότε φανήσεται ὁ κοσμοπλανὴς ὡς υἱὸς θεοῦ καὶ ποιήσει σημεῖα καὶ τέρατα, καὶ ἡ γῆ παραδοθήσεται εἰς χεῖρας αὐτοῦ, καὶ ποιήσει ἀθέμιτα, ἃ οὐδέποτε γέγονεν ἐξ αἰῶνος . . . καὶ τότε φανήσεται τὰ σημεῖα τῆς ἀληθείας.[11]

[10] *The Teaching of the Apostles* (London, 1887), p. 79.
[11] "For as lawlessness increases they shall hate one another and persecute and betray, and then shall appear the deceiver of the world as a Son of God, and shall do signs and wonders and the earth shall be given over into his hands and he shall commit iniquities which have never been since the world began. . . And then shall appear the signs of truth."

The similarity of this apocalyptic passage to the tenor of
Matthew xxiv and to certain Pauline details (cf. I Thessalonians iv.16; II Thessalonians ii.9) is at once suggestive,
but admits of no definite conclusion as to source. For there
is to be reckoned with an extensive reservoir of Jewish apocalyptic tradition basic to later Christian adaptation. For
present purposes, however, the question turns significantly,
not about the ultimate derivation of the utterances here recorded, but about the problem of the ascription of such
apocalyptic pronouncements to Jesus. This question has been
critically discussed elsewhere [12] and probabilities appear
evenly balanced. It would seem, nevertheless, that if Jesus
may be properly thought of as having given expression to
such sentiment, this expression must necessarily have been
secondary. Such enlargement upon and adaptation of canonical apocalyptic material as seems here evident, however, is
obviously in the interest of an ethical intensification of the
tone of daily Christian living.

Barnabas vi.13

λέγει δὲ κύριος· Ἰδοὺ ποιῶ τὰ ἔσχατα ὡς τὰ πρῶτα.[13]

Certainly any choice among the following texts would be
indecisive: Ezekiel xxxvi.11, Luke xiii.30 and parallels,
Revelation xxi.5. It seems probable, however, that the epistle
presents here less an independent saying of Jesus than a
loosely rewrought version of canonical materials identifiable
as to content if not as to form. Yet, it is because of this
mnemonic suggestiveness that we should here take account
less properly of deliberate emendation than of what seems
to be a characteristic confidence in the ethical and dogmatic

---

[12] Note especially the discussion set forth in Montefiore's *The Synoptic
Gospels* (2nd ed., rev.; London, 1927), I, 299ff.

[13] "And the Lord says, Behold, I make the last things as the first."

finality of supposed utterances of Jesus, however the formal
presentation.

Barnabas vii.11

οὖτως, φησίν, οἱ θέλοντές με ἰδεῖν καὶ ἅψασθαί μου τῆς βασιλείας
ὀφείλουσιν θλιβέντες καὶ παθόντες λαβεῖν με.[14]

This citation, paralleling in *The Shepherd of Hermas*
(Sim. vii.5) the principle of "attainment" (λαβεῖν) through
mandatory persecution (θλιβῆναί σε δεῖ), is further matched
in Gospels, in Acts, and in other early Christian literature by
similar phraseology. Resch concludes from this that a saying
of Jesus is probably basic to these renderings. Fatal to
this contention, however, seems the sober observation of
Ropes: "Anzunehmen, dass die Christen der zwei ersten
Jahrhunderte von Verfolgung und Drangsal nur auf Grund
eines Wortes Jesu reden konnten, scheint mir beinahe eine
Herzlosigkeit zu sein!"[15] On the other hand, it would be
difficult to overestimate the practical and religious values to
be derived from the conviction that Jesus himself endorsed
the spirit of the present pronouncement.

II Clement v.2–4

λέγει γὰρ ὁ κύριος· Ἔσεσθε ὡς ἀρνία ἐν μέσῳ λύκων· ἀποκριθεὶς δὲ ὁ
Πέτρος αὐτῷ λέγει· Ἐὰν οὖν διασπαράξωσιν οἱ λύκοι τὰ ἀρνία; εἶπεν ὁ
Ἰησοῦς τῷ Πέτρῳ· Μὴ φοβείσθωσαν τὰ ἀρνία τοὺς λύκους μετὰ
τὸ ἀποθανεῖν αὐτά· καὶ ὑμεῖς μὴ φοβεῖσθε τοὺς ἀποκτέννοντας ὑμᾶς καὶ
μηδὲν ὑμῖν δυναμένους ποιεῖν, ἀλλὰ φοβεῖσθε τὸν μετὰ τὸ ἀποθανεῖν
ὑμᾶς ἔχοντα ἐξουσίαν ψυχῆς καὶ σώματος, τοῦ βαλεῖν εἰς γέενναν πυρός.[16]

[14] "Thus, he says, Those who would see me and attain to my kingdom
must lay hold of me through pain and suffering."

[15] *Die Sprüche Jesu*, p. 8.

[16] "For the Lord said, You shall be as lambs in the midst of wolves; and
Peter answered and said to him, If then the wolves tear the lambs? Jesus
said to Peter, Let not the lambs fear the wolves after their death. And do

There is evident in this combination of Matthew x.16
(Luke x.3) with Matthew x.28 (Luke xii.4–5) an attempt to
furnish a continuous and harmonious context for these two
separate utterances. Professor Ropes thinks that the dialogue
represents rather a traditional form than an artfully conceived setting. It is also possible, however, to see in this an
effort, probably an early one, to come to grips with what
must have been an acute personal and social problem by
means of such recasting and enlargement of canonical sources
as are here apparent.

II Clement xii.2

ἐπερωτηθεὶς γὰρ αὐτὸς ὁ κύριος ὑπό τινος, πότε ἥξει αὐτοῦ ἡ βασιλεία,
εἶπεν· "Οταν ἔσται τὰ δύο ἕν, καὶ τὸ ἔξω ὡς τὸ ἔσω, καὶ τὸ ἄρσεν μετὰ
τῆς θηλείας οὔτε ἄρσεν οὔτε θῆλυ.[17]

This passage has been associated with a similar quotation
the source of which has been reasonably identified with the
heretical *Gospel According to the Egyptians*. To this document we shall later give fuller consideration. It seems likely,
however, that the writer of the Egyptian gospel, with its
tendentious additions, probably employed our present quotation to elaborate with his special details. Significantly, for
example, the anonymous interlocutor (cf. Luke xvii.20) is
there identified; the phrase "the outside as the inside" is
omitted, presumably to lend stronger support to the thesis
involved. On the other hand, Resch is probably right in
identifying II Clement's quotation with similar sentiment
from Ephesians (ii.14–16; iv.4–6), I Corinthians (xii.13),
Galatians (iii.28). The substance of the saying, therefore, is

---

not fear those that kill you and can do nothing else to you, but fear him
who after your death has power over soul and body, to cast them into
the Gehenna of fire."

[17] "For when the Lord himself was asked by someone when his kingdom
would come, he said, When the two shall be one, and the outside as the inside, and the male with the female neither male nor female."

evidently Pauline and the framework possibly Lucan (cf.
Luke xii.13; xvii.20; xviii.18). But Resch's conclusion that
the saying, like the Pauline utterances, owes its origin to
genuine words of Jesus is questionable. Quite the contrary,
the present religious emphasis upon the leveling of all bar-
riers as a prerequisite for the coming of the Kingdom seems
more easily accounted for on the view of conscious adaptation of available biblical matter.

Ignatius, Ad Smyrnaeos iii.2

ἔφη αὐτοῖς· Λάβετε, ψηλαφήσατέ με καὶ ἴδετε, ὅτι οὐκ εἰμὶ δαιμόνιον
ἀσώματον.[18]

Lagrange has shown good reason for believing that this is
probably not, as Resch believes, an original version of the
Hebrew gospel but a *jeu de mots* ("to which he [Ignatius]
was not averse") traceable to Ignatius' own invention.[19] Besson and others, on the contrary, have thought the quotation to represent "une forme plus ancienne de la parole du
Christ réssucité" (cf. Luke xxiv.39). It is to be noted, however, that Ignatius' anti-Docetic argument continues thus
(ii.1): ". . . but they are the ones who exist in semblance;
and, even as they think, so shall it happen that they will
have a mere bodiless (ἀσωμάτοις) and apparitional (δαι-
μονικοῖς) existence." Then follows the quotation as set forth
above.

By reason of the atmosphere of dire urgency in which Ignatius was forced to write, his citations have been seen to be
understandably summary and allusive (see pages 41–42).
Nevertheless, in view of the preoccupation as to rendering
which such "word play" implies, it seems reasonable to con-

[18] "He said to them, Take, handle me and see that I am not a bodiless
apparition."
[19] "L'Évangile selon les Hébreux," *Revue Biblique*, XXXI (July 1922),
325.

clude that we are here confronted with an intentional adaptation by Ignatius himself, conceived in the interest of his polemic.[20]

Justin Martyr, *Dialogus* 35

εἶπε γὰρ . . . ἔσονται σχίσματα καὶ αἱρέσεις.[21]

These words occur likewise in the *Didascalia* and in the *Clementine Homilies* as an utterance of Jesus. It is probable, however, that the context for this supposed saying is to be found in I Corinthians xi.18–19: "I hear that there are divisions [σχίσματα] among you . . . for there must also be factions [αἱρέσεις] among you. . ." It is thus perhaps more reasonable to assume hasty, allusive quotation on the part of Justin than to concur in the opinion that we have here to do with a genuine saying of Jesus. The instance is nevertheless instructive of the enhanced ethical appeal which was felt to attach to a sentiment set forth in the name of the Lord (εἶπε). Yet, this may be an occurrence simply of careless rather than of studied ascription.

Dialogus 47

ὁ ἡμέτερος κύριος Ἰησοῦς Χριστὸς εἶπεν· Ἐν οἷς ἂν ὑμᾶς καταλάβω, ἐν τούτοις καὶ κρινῶ.[22]

Resch shows thirteen instances of similar quotation in which the constant emphasis is upon "judgment." Possible

[20] Lagrange demonstrates convincingly Jerome's probable dependence (*De vir. ill.* 16) upon Eusebius (*H.E.* iii.36) in his mention of the present *logion*. Eusebius, in turn, presents his citation of these words as though from an unknown source. The Latin Origen (Rufinus: *De principiis* i. prooemium 8) quotes the same passage with uncertain reference to the *Doctrine of Peter*, against which, however, both document and reading, Origen (? Rufinus) immediately pronounces sweeping judgment. Such is the patristic confusion as to the source of this saying.

[21] "For he said, There shall be divisions and factions."

[22] "Our Lord Jesus Christ said, In whatever I apprehend you, in these things will I also judge you."

models have been adduced from Ezekiel xxxiii.20: "I will judge you [κρινῶ] each one after his own ways [ἐν ταῖς ὁδοῖς αὐτοῦ]"; xviii.30 similarly (reading κατά for ἐν). In all these patristic parallels, with but one exception, εὕρω (find) is read in the first clause; Justin is alone in reading καταλάβω (apprehend). Resch therefore conjectures, inconclusively it seems, that Justin's unique reading is the portion intended by him to represent the saying of "The Lord Jesus Christ." Later writers citing this dictum consider it an Old Testament utterance of Jehovah rather than a saying of Jesus. Further, many of these writers employ the saying either in direct connection with Ezekiel or confidently announce Ezekiel as its source. Whether these words stood in Pseudo-Ezekiel, Ropes points out, is also not proved. It appears, then, that the generally consistent quotation of this passage would argue for a documentary source. Since discussion of variation is thus impossible, it is nevertheless to be noted that profound ethical considerations prompted the creation of this sentiment and that again Justin has perhaps consciously enlisted the authority of Jesus in order to perpetuate its currency.

Irenaeus I.xx.2

πολλάκις ἐπεθύμησα ἀκοῦσαι ἕνα τῶν λόγων τούτων, καὶ οὐκ ἔσχον τὸν ἐροῦντα.[23]

It is extremely difficult to agree with Besson that this represents "Une parole dite sans doute par le Christ à l'occasion d'une déclaration de foi prononcée devant lui." [24] On the contrary, Resch is more cogent in the judgment: "Als Herrenwort gedacht, stellt dieses Logion in seiner gegenwärtigen Fassung geradezu eine Ungeheuerlichkeit dar, wenn

---

[23] "Many times have I desired to hear one of these words, and had no one to utter them."

[24] *Les Logia Agrapha* (Rouen, 1923), p. 122.

der Herr in dieser Weise von sich selbst geredet haben sollte."
Bishop Westcott has quite plausibly emended ἐπεθύμησα (I
desired) to read ἐπεθύμησαν (they desired), thus affording
a reasonable parallel, as Resch suggests, with Luke x.24
(Matthew xiii.17). Upon the acceptance of some such change,
one might indeed see in this dictum a typical Jewish expression of "longing for the coming of the Messiah." Again, if
canonical correspondence may be assumed, a religious attempt at heightened restatement (ἕνα τῶν λόγων κτλ — "*one
of these words, etc.*") of evangelic material may be reasonably argued from the emended quotation.

Clement of Alexandria, *Stromata* i.28

εἰκότως ἄρα καὶ ἡ γραφή . . . γίνεσθε δὲ δόκιμοι τραπεζῖται, τὰ μὲν
ἀποδοκιμάζοντες, τὸ δὲ καλὸν κατέχοντες.[25]

Professor Ropes indicates five independent witnesses, including Clement of Alexandria, for the currency of this *logion*
(in the shorter form) in Christian tradition. But the fact
that Origen (*Commentarius in Joannem* xix.2) recognized
the latter part of the quotation as words of Pauline origin
(I Thessalonians v.21) causes Ropes to infer that Clement
probably intended the same distinction in the present citation. Certainly the saying emerged in a Jewish environment
and survived actively only so long as the figure was relevant
to Jewish experience. An instructive parallel to this type of
thinking is seen in Philo (*De iudice*):[26] "And let the man
who undertakes the duty of a judge, like a skilful money-
changer [ἀργυραμοιβὸς ἀγαθός], divide and distinguish between the natures of things, in order that confusion may not
be caused by the mixing together of what is good [τὰ δόκιμα]
and what is spurious."[27] While this sentiment is not "de-

---

[25] "Rightly, therefore, the Scripture [says], Be skillful money-changers,
rejecting some things, but retaining what is good."
[26] *De specialibus legibus* IV.v.77.
[27] Translation that of C. D. Yonge.

cisive," it does furnish a reasonable basis for the judgment
that such a saying in Christian tradition is quite probably
derivative and secondary. Though this is not, then, an instance of textual variation, there is at stake a figure of ethical
force and persuasion for the early Christian community.

Stromata vi.5

διὰ τοῦτό φησιν ὁ Πέτρος εἰρηκέναι τὸν κύριον τοῖς ἀποστόλοις· ἐὰν μὲν
οὖν τις θελήσῃ τοῦ Ἰσραὴλ μετανοήσας διὰ τοῦ ὀνόματός μου πιστεύειν
ἐπὶ τὸν θεόν, ἀφεθήσονται αὐτῷ αἱ ἁμαρτίαι. μετὰ δώδεκα ἔτη ἐξέλθετε
εἰς τὸν κόσμον μή τις εἴπῃ· οὐκ ἠκούσαμεν.[28]

In keeping with an early Christian tradition according a
special importance to the eleventh (or twelfth) year after
the ascension of Christ, Acts i.4 is thus adapted to this unique
chronology from the *Preaching of Peter*. Nicephorus Callisti,
a fourteenth-century writer, records an interesting sequence
of events on the authority of one Bishop Euodius (*Historia
evangelica* ii.3), which probably represents an elaboration
in harmony with a similar body of ideas: "A baptismo usque
ad passionem Christi intercessisse annos tres: a passione
vero, resurrectione, et ascensione eius in coelos, usque ad
lapidationem Stephani annos septem: a Stephani deinde
martyrio, usque dum Paulum lux circumfudit, menses
sex. . ." [29]

As to our fragment, it seems well to conclude with Ropes,
"Das Stück will offenbar den Übergang des Christentums
von den Juden zu den Heiden als von Christus beabsichtigt
darstellen."

---

[28] "Therefore Peter says that the Lord said to the apostles: If, then, any
one of Israel wishes to repent, and through my name to believe in God, his
sins shall be forgiven him. After twelve years go out into the world, that no
one may say, We did not hear."

[29] Cf. Codex Askew: "Jesum post ascensionem suam in coelum iterum in
terram descendisse et undecim annis discipulos suos in variis mysteriis erudi-
visse atque — Philippo, Thomae et Matthaeo eum mandasse, ut dicta et
facta sua hoc intervallo temporis audita et visa scriptis connotarent."

Tertullian, *De Baptismo* 20

*Nam et praecesserat dictum: Neminem intentatum regna coelestia
consecuturum.*

The *Didascalia* presents this quotation but gives as its
source only "Scripture." If, however, the saying is to be
traced to a scriptural origin, James i.12–13 approximates
most nearly the thought involved. Certainly from the vague-
ness of the ascription in the *Didascalia* not much can be
argued, but the authority of Jesus would probably have been
appealed to if the writer knew a dominical pronouncement
to be involved. It seems likely, however, that such a maxim
might easily have grown out of the practical exigencies of
early Christian experience; although biblical utterances are
available which might reasonably account for its limits (cf.
also James i.2–3; I Peter i.6–7).

Origen, *Commentarius in Matthaeum* xiii.2

καὶ Ἰησοῦς γοῦν φησιν· διὰ τοὺς ἀσθενοῦντας ἠσθένουν καὶ διὰ τοὺς
πεινῶντας ἐπείνων καὶ διὰ τοὺς διψῶντας ἐδίψων.[30]

Resch and Ewald declare in favor of the genuineness of
this quotation as representing actual words of Jesus. Matthew
xxv.35–36, where the key words "hunger" (ἐπείνασα),
"thirst" (ἐδίψησα), and "sickness" (ἠσθένησα) appear in
consecutive clauses, perhaps affords a real basis for this conviction. Yet, with equal probability, I Corinthians ix.22
similarly suggests itself as a source of influence bearing upon
the form in which this dictum is cast. And since, at this point,
Pauline dependence upon extraneous sources cannot be
proved, it seems more reasonable to conclude, in the light
of available data, that Origen has probably supplemented a

---

[30] "And Jesus therefore said: Because of the sick I was sick, and because
of the hungry, I was hungry, and because of the thirsty I did thirst."

Pauline framework with Matthean details in an explanatory paraphrase. In fact, such an explicatory interest seems
basic to his context.

Origen, *Homilia in Jeremiam* xx.3

Διό φησιν ὁ σωτήρ· ῾Ο ἐγγύς μου ἐγγὺς τοῦ πυρός· ὁ δὲ μακρὰν ἀπ᾽
ἐμοῦ μακρὰν ἀπὸ τῆς βασιλείας.[31]

If "fire" in this context refers properly, as Ropes thinks,
to persecution, it is possible that we have in this alleged
saying of Jesus an attempt of the kind noted elsewhere (see
above, pp. 81 f., 88) to reconcile the fact of suffering with
normal Christian experience. As to probable parallels to
this quotation, Luke iii.16, xii.49, and Mark xii.34 may be
noted. Significant, perhaps, is Origen's own reserve concerning the authority of the utterance. He explains, in introduc-
ing the present *logion*: "Legi alicubi quasi Salvatore dicente,
et quaero, sive quis personam figuravit Salvatoris sive in
memoriam adduxit, an verum sit hoc, quod dictum est. . ."
Such hesitancy would not seem to justify a more confident
contemporary appraisal. Indeed, the apparently composite
features of this dictum prompt a reasonable doubt regarding
its supposed origin. It is, however, obvious that its currency,
as in other instances considered, argues eloquently for the
early Christian stress upon aphorisms of comfort and hope
felt to be consonant with the spirit of the Christ of the four
Gospels.

A discerning commentary upon the foregoing material is
offered by Professor Ropes. On the whole, "the authors
of the First and Third Gospels gathered up practically all
that the church in general possessed of the traditions of the
life and teachings of Jesus Christ." [32] Yet the ethical and

[31] "Wherefore the Savior says, He that is near me is near the fire; but he
that is far from me is far from the kingdom."

[32] "Agrapha," *Hastings' Dictionary of the Bible*, extra vol., p. 344.

social needs of the Christian fellowship were expanding and acute. Variations of canonical pronouncements, as well as independent didactic creations, were therefore extensively set forth and guaranteed by "thus saith the Lord" (λέγει Ἰησοῦς) the more forthrightly to meet these conditions. For the inspiration of the now risen Lord was felt to be continuously operative in the Christian community, insuring thus a continuing conformity, in the growing pattern of Christian life and thought, to the terms of the will of God.

XI

Jewish-Christian Gospels

A. EBIONITE FRAGMENTS

In examining the impress of early heterodox interests upon orthodox biblical patterns of thought, we might consider first those excerpts from the *Gospel of the Ebionites* which are found in Epiphanius' writings. According to Epiphanius, these fragments represent a mutilated form of Matthew and the total collection was called by its exponents the *Gospel According to the Hebrews*.

Epiphanius, *Adversus Haereses* xxx.13 (Cf. Matthew iv.13, ix.9, x.1–4)

καὶ ἐλθὼν εἰς Καφαρναοὺμ εἰσῆλθεν εἰς τὴν οἰκίαν Σίμωνος τοῦ ἐπικληθέν-
τος Πέτρου, καὶ ἀνοίξας τὸ στόμα αὐτοῦ εἶπεν· Παρερχόμενος παρὰ τὴν
λίμνην Τιβεριάδος ἐξελεξάμην Ἰωάννην καὶ Ἰάκωβον, υἱοὺς Ζεβεδαίου,
καὶ Σίμωνα καὶ Ἀνδρέαν καὶ Θαδδαῖον καὶ Σίμωνα τὸν ζηλωτὴν καὶ
Ἰούδαν τὸν Ἰσκαριώτην, καὶ σὲ τὸν Ματθαῖον καθεζόμενον ἐπὶ τοῦ
τελωνίου ἐκάλεσα καὶ ἠκολούθησάς μοι. ὑμᾶς οὖν βούλομαι εἶναι
δεκαδύο ἀποστόλους εἰς μαρτύριον τοῦ Ἰσραήλ.[1]

It is to be observed from these fragments that the testimony of the gospel is to be addressed, with proper exclusive-

---

[1] "And coming into Capernaum he entered into the house of Simon who was called Peter, and opened his mouth and said: As I passed by the lake of Tiberias, I chose John and James, sons of Zebedee, and Simon and Andrew and Thaddeus and Simon the Zealot and Judas Iscariot, and I called you, Matthew, sitting at the tax office, and you followed me. You, therefore, I will to be twelve apostles for a testimony to Israel."

ness, to Israel. If Matthew is intended as the writer, the authority for his narrative is certainly furnished by the implied collaboration of the Twelve Apostles.[2] And their investiture is secured by Jesus' personally announced choice. Jewish-Christian apologetic is thus patent.

Adversus Haereses xxx.16

ἦλθον καταλῦσαι τὰς θυσίας, καὶ ἐὰν μὴ παύσησθε τοῦ θύειν, οὐ παύσεται ἀφ' ὑμῶν ἡ ὀργή.[3]

An anomalous but fundamental characteristic of these Jewish Christians was an uncompromising bias against the prophets of the Old Testament and against its sacramental system. The latter objection may be readily accounted for from their strictly vegetarian preferences (conceived on Encratite grounds). This being so, it is easy to discern the tendency evidenced by this saying.

Adversus Haereses xxx.14 (Matthew xii.48.50 and parallels)

τίς μού ἐστι μήτηρ καὶ ἀδελφοί; καὶ ἐκτείνας τὴν χεῖρα ἐπὶ τοὺς μαθητὰς ἔφη· οὗτοί εἰσιν οἱ ἀδελφοί μου καὶ ἡ μήτηρ καὶ ἀδελφαί οἱ ποιοῦντες τὰ θελήματα τοῦ πατρός μου.[4]

This passage is probably intended less as a denial of Jesus' manhood, according to Epiphanius' deduction, than as a support for still another special doctrinal tendency. The plural of the canonical "will" (θελήματα) is reasonably thought to recall the Old Testament commandments. The passage con-

---

[2] The balance of critical opinion, as Findlay notes (pp. 38f.), is probably correct in identifying the *Gospel of the Twelve Apostles* mentioned by Origen (*Hom. in Luc.* i.) with the Ebionite gospel.

[3] "I came to destroy the sacrifices, and unless you cease from sacrificing, the wrath [of God] will not cease from you."

[4] "Who is my mother and who are my brothers? And stretching out his hand toward his disciples, he said, These are my brothers and mother and sisters who do the will of my Father."

sequently advances a legalistic conception of religion in harmony with Jewish emphasis.

Adversus Haereses xxx.22 (Cf. Luke xxii.15)

Μὴ ἐπιθυμίᾳ ἐπεθύμησα κρέας τοῦτο τὸ Πάσχα φαγεῖν μεθ' ὑμῶν; [5]

Concordantly with their abstention from animal flesh on doctrinal grounds, κρέας (flesh) has been aptly inserted into the gospel text as indicated. The Passover observance, on Jesus' own authority, has therefore been clearly guarded against defilement by the eating of meat.

B. THE GOSPEL ACCORDING TO THE EGYPTIANS

A work of a purely secondary character is the *Gospel According to the Egyptians*, of which a few fragments may be gleaned from the writings of Clement of Alexandria. M. R. James notes the general pattern of the work to be consistent "with later Gnostic books such as the *Pistis Sophia* in assigning an important role in the dialogues with Christ to the female disciples." The peculiar tendency involved will be at once manifest.

Clement of Alexandria, *Stromata* iii.9,13

αὐτὸς εἶπεν ὁ σωτήρ· ἦλθον καταλῦσαι τὰ ἔργα τῆς θηλείας . . . ἡ Σαλώμη φησί· μέχρι τίνος οἱ ἄνθρωποι ἀποθανοῦνται; . . . ἀποκρίνεται ὁ κύριος· μέχρις ἂν τίκτωσιν αἱ γυναῖκες . . . πυνθανομένης τῆς Σαλώμης πότε γνωσθήσεται τὰ περὶ ὧν ἤρετο, ἔφη ὁ κύριος· ὅταν τὸ τῆς αἰσχύνης ἔνδυμα πατήσητε καὶ ὅταν γένηται τὰ δύο ἓν καὶ τὸ ἄρρεν μετὰ τῆς θηλείας οὔτε ἄρρεν οὔτε θῆλυ.[6]

[5] "Have I desired greatly to eat this flesh of the Passover with you?"

[6] "The Savior himself said: I came to destroy the works of the female. . . . Salome says, Until when shall men die? The Lord answers: So long as women bear children. When Salome inquired when the things concerning which she asked should be known, the Lord said: When you trample on the garment of shame and when the two become one and the male with the female is neither male nor female."

The Encratite thesis in the guise of dominical utterances
need not be further labored. Suffice it to say that Clement's
apologetic exegesis of the passage is scarcely to be squared
with what was apparently the author's intent. The relationship of this dialogue to a similar presentation in II Clement
has already been noted (see pp. 82 f.). That II Clement's
treatment of the source involved is a more faithful one, however, is probable in view of the present omissions and additions in support of specific interests.

C. THE GOSPEL ACCORDING TO THE HEBREWS [7]

The Gospel According to the Hebrews marks something of a departure from the apocryphal fragments hereto-
fore considered. Eusebius (*H.E.* iii.27) mentions it as being
current among what he distinguishes as the more orthodox
branch of Jewish Christians (Ebionites), although this sect,
too, revealed certain heterodox tendencies, according to Eusebius. They rejected the Apostle Paul and the belief in Jesus'
preëxistence, considering him a "mere man" (ψιλὸς ἄνθρωπος). Their Gospel of Matthew, on Epiphanius' authority
(*Haereses* xxix.9), was nevertheless "quite complete" — in
contrast to the "mutilated" Matthean version in use among
more radical believers. Besides the Gospel of Matthew, again
according to Eusebius (*H.E.* iii.27), "they regarded the others
of little value" (τῶν λοιπῶν σμικρὸν ἐποιοῦντο λόγον). It
will be seen, however, that even this perhaps purest of
Jewish-Christian gospel versions exhibits a pattern identical with that of other *antilegomena* in its studied conflation
and elaboration of an extensive body of canonical material.

---

[7] The selections are based on a critical compilation made by the Rev.
Père Lagrange, *Revue Biblique*, XXXI (1922), which treats the Nazarene
gospel and the *Gospel According to the Hebrews* as parts of the same document. Schmidtke and other competent scholars, however, do not make such
an identification.

Stromata ii.9; v.14

ὁ θαυμάσας βασιλεύσει, γέγραπται, καὶ ὁ βασιλεύσας ἀναπαήσεται . . .
οὐ παύσεται ὁ ζητῶν, ἕως ἂν εὕρῃ· εὑρὼν δὲ θαμβηθήσεται, θαμβηθεὶς
δὲ βασιλεύσει, βασιλεύσας δὲ ἐπαναπαήσεται.[8]

It will be seen that this saying as quoted by Clement (in
its longer form) corresponds almost exactly to Saying I of the
Oxyrhynchus *Logia* — the initial clause in the "sayings"
source being an injunction. We shall discuss later the inferences drawn from this coincidence. For the moment we may
observe Clement's association of the idea of "wonderment"
with the Platonic proposition set forth in the *Theaetetus*
(*Stromata* ii.9), although this provides no clue concerning its
origin. A corresponding notion may be detected in II Clement
(v.5): "The promise of Christ is great and wonderful and
brings us rest, in the kingdom which is to come and in everlasting life." [9] It is conceivable, then, that in our present
saying the idea of wonderment might bear some such suggestion as "the promise of Christ" (cf. I Corinthians ii.9). Significance perhaps attaches to the fact that the notion of
"wonder," "resting," and the suggestion of "reigning"
(βασιλείας) recorded by II Clement correspond roughly
to the sequence in Clement of Alexandria's presentation.
Thus it is probable that, although the saying as a whole is a
new one, its component parts stem for the most part from
biblical sources. The suggestion of "seeking" and "finding"
is present in Matthew vii.7 (and parallels). The thought of
"resting" and of "reigning," apocalyptically conceived, finds
frequent mention in the text of the New Testament; Romans
v.17, II Timothy ii.12, Hebrews iv.9, and Revelation, *pas-*

[8] "It is written: He that has wondered shall reign and he that has reigned
shall rest . . . He who seeks will not cease till he find; and having found,
he shall wonder; and having wondered he shall reign; and reigning he
shall rest."

[9] So rendered by Lake, Loeb Classical Library.

sim, are but a few of many instances of their occurrence.
Hence the saying derives probably from a homiletic enlargement upon familiar material within an area of experience frequently contemplated in early Christianity.

Origen, *Commentarius in Joannem* ii.12

Ἐὰν δὲ προσιῆταί τις τὸ καθ' Ἑβραίους εὐαγγέλιον, ἔθνα αὐτὸς ὁ σωτήρ
φησιν· Ἄρτι ἔλαβέ με ἡ μήτηρ μου, τὸ ἅγιον πνεῦμα, ἐν μιᾷ τῶν τριχῶν
μου καὶ ἀπήνεγκέ με εἰς τὸ ὄρος τὸ μέγα Θαβώρ.¹⁰

We apparently have here to do with a bold adaptation of
the story of the Temptation. Ezekiel viii.3 seems likely
to have prompted the metaphor. If, as Evelyn White thinks
(*The Sayings of Jesus*, Introduction, pp. lxiv–lxv), there is
observable a consistent effort in the Hebrew gospel to find
Messianic fulfillment in as many Old Testament passages as
possible, Psalm lxxxix.13 and Jeremiah xlvi.18 may very well
be responsible for the reference to Mount Tabor, though in-
appropriately selected on other grounds.¹¹ Attention has
been called to the contrast presented by the harshness of the
Marcan expulsion (i.12) and the very sensitive dealing of
the Spirit in our present version. Thus a dogmatic softening
and reinterpretation of the canonical account seems un-
doubtedly present.

Eusebius, *Theophania* iv.12

He [Christ] taught the reason for the division of souls which
was to occur in families, as we have found somewhere in the gospel
current among the Jews in the Hebrew language, where it is said:

¹⁰ "And if any accept the Gospel according to the Hebrews, where the
Savior himself says: Even now my mother the Holy Spirit took me by one
of my hairs, and carried me away to the great mountain Tabor."
¹¹ Dr. Adeney observes here the inappropriateness of reference to Mt.
Tabor as the site of the Temptation by reason of its use as a Roman fortress
in the time of Jesus (*Hibbert Journal*, III [1904], 150ff.).

"I choose for myself the best that my Father in heaven gives me."[12]

An excellent example of the composite character of this document is afforded by the present saying. The Synoptic setting seems obvious — Matthew x.35–37. Johannine details are to be seen in the apparent conflation of sentiment similar to John xiii.18 and xvii.6. The "alien" element felt by Evelyn White, however, revolving presumably about the assertion "I have chosen the best . . ." is probably an orthodox attempt to interpret John xiii.18, with possible recollections of Matthew xxii.14, rather than an advocacy of heterodox principles.

Theophania iv.1

τὸ . . . Ἑβραϊκοῖς χαρακτῆρσιν εὐαγγέλιον τὴν ἀπειλὴν οὐ κατὰ τοῦ ἀποκρύψαντος ἐπῆγεν, ἀλλὰ κατὰ τοῦ ἀσώτως ἐζηκότος· τρεῖς γὰρ δούλους περιεῖχε, τὸν μὲν καταφαγόντα τὴν ὕπαρξιν τοῦ δεσπότου μετὰ πορνῶν καὶ αὐλητρίδων, τὸν δὲ πολλαπλασιάσαντα τὴν ἐργασίαν, τὸν δὲ κατακρύψαντα τὸ τάλαντον· εἶτα τὸν μὲν ἀποδεχθῆναι, τὸν δὲ μεμφθῆναι μόνον, τὸν δὲ συγκλεισθῆναι δεσμωτηρίῳ.[13]

The Hebrew gospel in its evident departure from canonical Matthew aims here apparently at tempering the judgment pronounced against the indolent servant recorded in Matthew xxv.30. The tableau is that of Matthew xxv.14–30. The account of the wicked servant (which Eusebius conjectures to refer properly to Matthew xxiv.48–51) reveals obvious

[12] So rendered from the French of Lagrange (*Revue Biblique*, XXXI [1922], 176), which is based, in turn, upon Gressmann's translation from the Syriac.

[13] "The gospel written in Hebrew characters turned the threat not against him who had hid the talent but against the one who had lived riotously — for it told of three servants, one who devoured the master's substance with harlots and flute-girls, another who multiplied it by trading, and another who hid the talent; then made the one to be accepted, another only rebuked, and another to be shut up in prison."

borrowings from the story of the Prodigal Son (Luke xv.13, 30). In this composite setting, therefore, an apologetic interest relative to the ethical sanctions of Christian experience appears evident.

Origen, In Matthaeum xix.16

Quod dicitur secundum Hebraeos . . . dixit, inquit, ad eum alter divitum: Magister, quid bonum faciens vivam? Dixit ei: Homo, leges et prophetas fac. Respondit ad eum: Feci. Dixit ei: Vade, vende omnia quae possides et divide pauperibus, et veni, sequere me. Coepit autem dives scalpere caput suum et non placuit ei. Et dixit ad eum Dominus: Quomodo dicis: legem feci et prophetas? quoniam scriptum est in lege: diliges proximum tuum sicut te ipsum; et ecce multi fratres tui, filii Abrahae, amicti sunt stercore, morientes prae fame, et domus tua plena est multis bonis, et non egreditur omnino aliquid ex ea ad eos. . .

A Matthean framework (xix.16–26) is at once recognizable in this excerpt. On the other hand, Lucan reminiscences are likewise not far to seek. Parallels to the Lucan parable (Luke xvi) which Evelyn White notes include the following: *alter divitum* (Luke: "there was a certain rich man"); *filii Abrahae* (Luke: Father Abraham); *amicti sunt stercore* (Luke: "who was clothed in purple and fine linen"); *domus tua plena est bonis* (Luke: "feasted sumptuously every day"); *morientes prae fame* (Luke: "desired to be fed with what fell from the rich man's table").

In addition to the fondness for conflation, there is also an apologetic interest manifest in some of these fragments. It may be noted, for example, that the "counsel of perfection" given in canonical Matthew (xix.21) seems to imply a real advance upon the legal injunctions imposed. Quite awkwardly, therefore, has this tirade of Jesus' been inserted after the *vade vende omnia* . . . in our present version. The clear purpose of this is, of course, to prove that "keeping the law and the prophets" itself entails radical self-abnegation and is thus adequate to fulfill all righteousness.

Jerome, *De Viris Illustribus* 2

Evangelium quoque, quod appellatur secundum Hebraeos . . . refert: Dominus autem cum dedisset sindonem servo sacerdotis, ivit ad Iacobum et apparuit ei (iuraverat enim Iacobus se non comesurum panem ab illa hora, qua biberat calicem Domini donec videret eum resurgentem a dormientibus); rursusque post paululum: Adferte, ait Dominus, mensam et panem; statimque additur: Tulit panem et benedixit et fregit et dedit Iacobo iusto et dixit ei: Frater mi, comede panem tuum, quia resurrexit Filius hominis a dormientibus.

It is scarcely possible that this account of the resurrection would be capable of superseding our earliest canonical reference (I Corinthians xv). Special interests are here unmistakably evident. James is now "the Just" — an obvious instance of later accretion. In refutation of Jewish calumny, a servant of the high priest is made the first witness of the resurrection. And the "tangible" appearance to James takes precedence over appearances to the other disciples. James is thus seen to have been a believer before Jesus' death — facts which, relative to our document, constitute "the clearest manifestation of a Jewish-Christian spirit." Further, *tulit panem* . . . in its resemblance to Luke xxiv.30 (Matthew xxvi.26), as well as James' vow, reminiscent of Acts xxiii.12, argues probable indebtedness of this striking account to canonical sources.

Jerome, *Dialogus adversus Pelagianos* iii.2

Ecce mater Domini et fratres eius dicebant ei: Ioannes Baptista baptizat in remissionem peccatorum: eamus et baptizemur ab eo. Dixit autem eis: Quid peccavi, ut vadam et baptizer ab eo? Nisi forte hoc ipsum quod dixi, ignorantia est.

A dogmatic concern over the problem presented by the acceptance of the "sinless Christ" of a baptism of repentance for remission of sins may be detected in this passage. It is now clear that Jesus acceded to the rite, not because of a personal persuasion of sin, but in response to a request from his mother and his brothers. The difficult *nisi forte . . .* probably anticipates any charge of ignorance by its implied denial. The purpose of the extract, nevertheless, does not turn on this appendage, which, however it be interpreted, is certainly calculated to reinforce rather than to detract from the stature of the personality thus depicted.

Dialogus adversus Pelagianos iii.2

Et in eodem volumine: Si peccaverit, inquit, frater tuus in verbo, et satis tibi fecerit, septies in die suscipe eum. Dixit illi Simon, discipulus eius: Septies in die? Respondit Dominus et dixit ei: Etiam ego dico tibi, usque septuagies septies. Etenim in prophetis quoque postquam uncti sunt spiritu sancto, inventus est sermo peccati.[14]

This fragment is hardly offered by way of improvement upon Matthew xviii.21–22, although the specification of verbal sin should be noted. Here, as elsewhere, there seems to exist a pointed contrast between Christ and the prophets. For example, the sentiment thus recorded — "Descendit super eum omnis fons spiritus sancti . . . Fili mi, in omnibus prophetis expectabam te ut venires"[15] — is not inconsistent with the present thesis, which indicates clearly the relatively imperfect endowment of the Holy Spirit upon the prophets as over against Christ.

[14] Lagrange thinks *sermo peccati* to be a Hebraism for "any sin."
[15] Jerome, *Comm. in Is.* iv.11.

Jerome, *Commentarius in Ezechielem* xviii.7

*In evangelio, quod iuxta Hebraeos Nazaraei legere consueverunt,
inter maxima ponitur crimina, qui fratris sui spiritum contrista-
verit.*

The origin of this sentiment is not known. Ezekiel xviii.7,
however, has been thought to be the point of departure for
the saying; nevertheless, the identification cannot be pressed.
Matthew v.22 presents also a plausible parallel; nor is it
impossible to detect here a "Johannine ring." Since localiza-
tion is not possible, it may be said that the sentiment is
neither "old" nor "new" but represents, despite its probable
secondary character, a quality not unworthy of an utterance
of Jesus nor yet inferior to the tenderer prophetic ideals.

Jerome, *Commentarius in Ephesios* v.4

*In Hebraico quoque evangelio legimus Dominum ad discipulos
loquentem: Et numquam, inquit, laeti sitis, nisi cum fratrem
vestrum videritis in caritate.*

Matthew v.24 and xviii.15ff. are near parallels to this excerpt, though the resemblance is one of spirit rather than of
form. Evelyn White sees here also a possible Johannine
"coloring." It is indeed probable that we have here a homiletic "exaggeration" of evangelic sentiment, and so a saying
derivative rather than original in its expression.

Jerome, *Commentarius in Matthaeum* vi.11

*In evangelio, quod appellatur Secundum Hebraeos, pro super-
substantiali pane, reperi* Mahar, *quod dicitur crastinum. . .*

It is difficult, in view of the secondary features noted in
this gospel, to regard *mahar* (tomorrow) as an original rendering in Matthew vi.11, though the possibility must be ad-

mitted. It seems probable, on the other hand, that *mahar* represents rather a conjecture regarding the sense of the difficult ἐπιούσιος (daily) — a possibility that is in keeping with the liberties taken elsewhere with the text of canonical Matthew by the editors of the Hebrew gospel. On the supposition, however, that *mahar* is the better reading for this text, Findlay's objection "that a word so puzzling in its form and meaning as ἐπιούσιος should have been used to translate *mahar*, when a simpler expression was available" [16] seems pertinent.[17]

[16] Findlay, p. 75.

[17] Of interest are the marginal glosses edited by Schmidtke from certain manuscripts (for the most part, von Soden's δ30) where they are found listed under the heading Tὸ 'Ιουδαϊκόν. It is thought that "the Jewish" gospel refers to our present gospel. εἰκῆ may be noted here as an original reading from Mt. v.22 (cf. Appendix C). Matthew vii.5 reads: "Though you be on my bosom and do not the will of my Father in heaven, I will cast you forth from my bosom." Schmidtke has pointed out the more appropriate application of this variant to the thought in verses 21–23. There is also involved a possible allusion to Jn. xiii.23. In any case, the emphasis intended here is probably upon a predominantly legalistic conception of Christianity — a glorification of works compatible with other sentiment in this gospel. For Mt. x.16, the gloss reads "more than (ὑπὲρ) serpents" instead of "as (ὡς) serpents." In Mt. xii.40, the words "three days and three nights" are omitted. Lagrange queries: "Parce que ces mots ont paru inutiles? ou pour ne pas trop insister sur les trois jours et les trois nuits avant la résurrection?"

XII

The Oxyrhynchus Sayings of Jesus [1]

In Appendix A of this monograph, the author has attempted to show that the Oxyrhynchus *Logia* (Papyri 1, 654) reveal a pattern of development which might plausibly be associated with a homiletic genre of expression. There seem several reasons why this is probably so. Certainly the dramatic quality of these excerpts may be easily conceded. To be sure, this feature has been elsewhere adduced, quite apart from the present homiletic hypothesis, to connect the collection with other extant fragments. [2] On the other hand, the derivative tone of these sayings has been noted by investigators from the very first. Among other possible sources, our canonical Gospels have been consistently detected to be basic to the Oxyrhynchus compilation. It has seemed safe to infer upon further consideration, therefore, that we have to do with an expansion of essentially evangelic material with what seems best identified as sermonic intent. Again, the doctrinally neutral character of these dicta appears reasonably evident — a feature which has also received significantly uniform recognition by scholars. Hence visible departures

[1] This discussion appeared originally as an article in the *London Quarterly and Holborn Review*, XVIII (1949), 158–161. The author is grateful to the editor of that journal for permission to reproduce this material here.

[2] H. G. Evelyn White's edition of the Oxyrhynchus *Logia* is here used as the basic text. In his careful Introduction, Evelyn White argues definite literary relationship between the *Gospel According to the Hebrews* and the *Logia* by reason of their commonly "striking and dramatic" traits.

from the limits of canonical expression seem accounted for
with least difficulty on the ground of deliberate, homiletic
elaboration, within which hortatory and didactic framework
the "striking and dramatic," so consistently present in these
fragments, is the normal concomitant.

The disposition to see in any of the Oxyrhynchus sayings
possibly "an earlier and more original version" than its
canonical counterpart [3] thus appears less probable by way
of explanation of their unique character than the application
of the principle here suggested. Also, on this consideration,
wherever canonical basis can be reasonably asserted, there
may be observed the attempt, not to quote slavishly our four
Gospels, but to weave freely their phrases and spirit into an
original fabric, with the probable aim of embodying the authority of their suggestion rather than capturing the accuracy
of their form.

Modern scholarship in some of its most responsible pronouncements has made out impressively credible cases for
provenance in the suggestion of one or another of the extant
apocryphal gospels. The discoverers' choice of the *Gospel
According to the Egyptians* [4] and Harnack's more elaborate
arguments for the same source [5] need simply be mentioned.
As already intimated, H. G. Evelyn White has demonstrated
preference for the *Gospel According to the Hebrews* as the
probable matrix for our present materials.[6] Or the attempt
has been made, as by Charles Taylor,[7] to set forth a number
of possible sources. He, too, however, sees in the *Gospel According to the Egyptians* the most probable context from
which these fragments might have been appropriated. It
should nevertheless be noted that, even in terms of treatment

[3] So Evelyn White with reference to Saying VI.

[4] Grenfell and Hunt, *Sayings of Our Lord* (London, 1897).

[5] *Über die jüngst entdeckten Sprüche Jesu* (Leipzig und Tübingen, 1897).

[6] *The Sayings of Jesus from Oxyrhynchus* (Cambridge, England, 1920).

[7] *The Oxyrhynchus Logia and the Apocryphal Gospels* (London, 1899).

of this latter sort, canonical sayings are felt to be fundamental to the logographer's elaboration.[8]

As to the character of the *Logia*, we might well reëmpha-
size here what Grenfell and Hunt realized from the beginning. Initial and later observations concur in judging these
fragments to be conspicuously devoid of tendency. This fact
is patently in contrast to the "clear manifestations of a Jewish-Christian spirit" attaching to the *Gospel According to
the Hebrews*; nor do the few Encratite fragments from the
Gospel According to the Egyptians, alongside the Oxyrhynchus collection, argue more harmonious rapport. Saying I,[9] duplicated almost verbatim in the Hebrew gospel, admittedly, gives sober pause. The coincidence, however, does
not seem unequivocally to sustain the conclusion of literary
identity for the two sources in view of the equally urgent
alternatives by which such similarity might be explained.
For, as we have seen, a suggestion of the same *seriatim* arrangement of ideas in II Clement (v.5) as is common to the
Hebrew gospel and the *Logia* points to the possibility of an
identical source, or to similar sources, for all three documents. Certainly the Syriac rendering of the *Acts of Thomas*
("And when he hath found rest he becometh a king"),[10] in
addition to various New Testament treatments of the apocalyptic themes "resting" and "reigning," indicates a familiar
currency of these ideas in early Christianity, either singly
or in the combinations presented above. In any case, identi-

[8] Kirsopp Lake ("The New Sayings of Jesus," *Hibbert Journal*, III
[1905], 332ff.) opposes the opinion of W. Sanday that the development of
the *Logia* parallels that of our canonical Gospels. Dr. Lake nonetheless does
feel that these sayings illustrate the growth of gospel tradition with its
twofold and, as often, independent interest in "sayings" and "doings."

[9] Saying I and corresponding Hebrew fragment present the identical
sequence: "seeking," "finding," "amazement," "reigning," "rest"; II Clement
approximates this order with the notion of "wonder," ($\theta\alpha\upsilon\mu\alpha\sigma\tau\dot{\eta}$), of "resting," and the suggestion of "reigning" ($\beta\alpha\sigma\iota\lambda\epsilon\dot{\iota}\alpha\varsigma$).

[10] W. Wright, *Apocryphal Acts* (London, 1871), p. 270.

fication of *Logia* and Hebrew gospel need not necessarily turn about their mutual possession of the saying under discussion.

If, on the other hand, it can be established that in the Oxyrhynchus *Logia* we have to do with a set of pregnant sayings of Jesus which have been homiletically elaborated, interest would seem to attach anew to what has been early observed to be a probable point of correspondence between our present fragments and certain areas of the *Corpus Hermeticum*. It will be noted that Saying VIII and *Corp*. VII (1, 2) reveal a striking similarity in sentiment. Associating "blindness" and "ignorance," they imply "drunkenness" to be basic to both. It is at once obvious how guarded any conclusion must be which might follow from such agreement. Yet the juxtaposition of "blindness" and "ignorance" is at least a suggestive point of contact between the two writings. On the other hand, Eusebius' similar quotation in *Adversus Hieroclem* [11] points to the availability and the appeal of this Hermetic sentiment, or its sources, to Christian protagonists. What seems significant, however, is the unmistakably homiletic tone and pattern of Hermetic and Oxyrhynchus excerpts at this juncture — a tone and pattern here felt to be easily demonstrable throughout the Oxyrhynchus collection as thus far recovered.

Of the spirit of this particular "sermonette" Dibelius remarks significantly: "Such a combination of self recommendation and of the preaching of conversion is the typical mark of the divine or semi-divine herald of a revelation in Hellenistic religiousness, i.e. of a mythological person. In these ways speak sons of God and supermen who promise the world the only true salvation. . . In the churches . . . the person of Jesus was looked upon in the light of this redemption faith." [12]

[11] Chap. 42.
[12] *From Tradition to Gospel* (New York, 1935), pp. 281ff.

Whether λέγει Ἰησοῦς (Jesus says) can be supported as the guarantee for the solemn pronouncement of a Hellenistic "superman" in Christian guise need not be labored. It does seem defensible to assert that the hortatory impression appears similarly persistent upon both Oxyrhynchus and Hermetic details. Indeed, Hermes says: "I made myself a guide to mankind, teaching them the doctrine, how in what wise they might be saved. And I sowed in them the teachings of wisdom; and that which I sowed was watered with the water of immortal life. . ." [13] Nor can it be seriously questioned that, methodologically, the authority of Jesus has in the *Logia* been likewise enlisted to some such end.

There is here no inclination to identify the Sayings of Jesus with the theosophical-philosophical literature of Hermes. This writer is nevertheless tempted to conjecture an acquaintance on the part of the Christian logographer with the Hermetic writings. Such a possible acquaintance may thus be reflected in his studied use and hortatory elaboration of essentially evangelic sources, countering consciously the esoteric pronouncements of Hermes with the "life-giving" sayings of Jesus.

[13] *Corpus Hermeticum*, I.29 (Walter Scott, *Hermetica* [Oxford, 1924], Vol. I).

XIII

Papyrus Egerton 2

In 1935, H. I. Bell and T. C. Skeat brought to the attention of scholars some papyrological fragments of what was thought to be an "Unknown Gospel." These fragments, which are known as Papyrus Egerton 2, have since that time received exhaustive investigation. The definitive work to date, however, has been a monograph by Dr. Goro Mayeda (*Das Leben-Jesu-Fragment, Papyrus Egerton 2*, Berne, 1946), whose original research in this area was in the form of a doctoral dissertation written under Professor Martin Dibelius of Heidelberg. An excellent review of this monograph was written by Bell for the express purpose of making available Mayeda's findings to British and American scholarship ("The Gospel Fragments Papyrus Egerton 2," *Harvard Theological Review*, XLII [1949], 53–63). In view of Mayeda's exhaustive treatment of this papyrus, nothing more is attempted here than a summary presentation of his reported conclusions, along with such comments as the findings of this present monograph may suggest. For perspective, however, it may be well to review a few representative opinions bearing upon the papyrus.

At the outset, Bell and Skeat, identified the papyrological fragments as "indubitably a real gospel . . . sober, concise, matter-of-fact." They dated it as falling "somewhat later than the middle of the second century." In an elaborated opinion set forth in his article, Bell states further, using Mayeda's terminology: "By 'Gospel' we did not mean 'eine Schrift, die zur Verkündigung und Verbreitung der Botschaft dient,' but merely a real narrative of the life and teaching of Jesus as against either a collection of sayings or a mosaic of Gospel excerpts." Of Synoptic dependence the editors could find no clear trace, points of resemblance between Eg. (abbreviation adopted by Bell) and the Synoptics being so remote that they were felt probably to represent independent traditions. Similarity to the Fourth Gospel is such, on the contrary, that they advanced the following possibilities to account for agreements: Johannine dependence upon Eg.; dependence of the writer of Eg. upon John; dependence of both writers upon a common source.

As to other opinions bearing upon these fragments, it should be noted that H. S. Shelton, writing in the *Hibbert Journal* (XLIII [1945], 157–162), supports strongly the view that they constitute one of the sources of the Fourth Gospel. Robert Casey (*American Journal of Philology*, LVII [1936], 103–107) thinks that we have here to do with an "unmotivated harmony" of our four Gospels. Kirsopp Lake (*Religion in Life*, V [1936], 101), however, expresses "skepticism as to the arguments Professor Casey produces as to the secondary nature of the text in these fragments, as compared with the Canonical Gospels, because . . . such arguments can generally be reversed. It is very hard to say, especially in dealing with more or less illiterate documents, whether the better or the worse reading has the greater claim to be accepted." Lake himself suggests a possible identification of Eg. with the *Gospel According to the Hebrews*. He does not, however, press such an identification. Among continental scholars, Hans Lietzmann's conviction as to the apocryphal quality of these fragments should also be mentioned (*ZNW*, XXXIV [1935], 285 ff.), in addition to Joachim Jeremias' opinion (*Junge Kirche*, VI [1938], 572–582) suggesting their derivative character and the probable importance of memory as a factor in their creation.

There follows a translation of Eg. by Bell in accordance with his own textual reconstruction. Only those episodes embodying the words of Jesus are reproduced here.

I. A CONVERSATION WITH THE RULERS OF THE PEOPLE

. . . (1) And Jesus said unto the lawyers, Punish every wrong-doer and transgressor, and not me. For if . . . doeth, how doth he do it? (2) And turning to the rulers of the people he spake this saying, Search the scriptures, in which ye think that ye have life; these are they which bear witness of me [John v.39]. (3) Think not that I came to accuse you to my Father; there is one that accuseth you, even Moses, on whom ye have set your hope [John v.45]. (4) And when they said, We know well that God spake unto Moses, but as for thee, we know not whence thou art [John ix.29], Jesus answered and said unto them, Now is your unbelief accused. . .

II. THE HEALING OF A LEPER

(8) And behold, there cometh to him a leper and saith, Master Jesus, journeying with lepers and eating with them in the inn I myself also became a leper. If therefore thou wilt, I am made clean. (9) The Lord then said unto him, I will; be thou made clean. And straightway the leprosy departed from him [Matthew viii.2–4; Mark i.40–44; Luke v.12–14]. (10) And the Lord said unto him, Go thy way and show thyself unto the priests [Luke xvii.14].

III. THE QUESTION OF THE TEMPTERS

. . . (11) coming unto him began to tempt him with a question, saying, Master Jesus, we know that thou art come from God [John iii.2], for the things which thou doest testify above all the prophets [John x.25]. (12) Tell us therefore: Is it lawful to render unto kings those things which pertain unto their rule?

Shall we render unto them, or not? (13) But Jesus, knowing their
thought [Matthew xxii.17–18; Mark xii.14–15; Luke xx.22–23],
being moved with indignation, said unto them, Why call ye me
with your mouth Master, when ye hear not what I say [Luke
vi.46]? (14) Well did Isaiah prophesy of you, saying, This people
honour me with their lips, but their heart is far from me. In vain
do they worship me, teaching as their doctrines the precepts of
men . . . [Matthew xv.7–9; Mark vii.6–7].

In Section I, Bell presents a key argument of Mayeda's to
explain "one of the chief problems raised by the fragments,
that, on the one hand, Synoptic incidents are related with
marked material differences from the Synoptists, and, on the
other, Johannine sayings appear in a setting which verbally
accords better with the Synoptic style." In the first place,
there may be noted the imperative "search" for "you
search" [1] and the relative clause "in which" for the causal
"because." Mayeda suggests here that Eg. probably presents the original and John an adapted rendering of the
source involved. For, he continues, "der Imperativ mit ἐν
αἷς ist vulgärer. . . Der Indicativ mit ὅτι ist johanneischer."
Following Dibelius' lead in recognizing a "vorjohannei-
schen Eindruck" in these fragments, Mayeda holds it to be
probable that "John . . . was using, in his individual way,
materials on which Eg. was probably drawing quite independently." The presence of "eternal life" in the parallel
Johannine version is felt at this point to illustrate intrinsically the independence, or priority, of the papyrological
rendering, or its source, in reference to John. As the passage
continues, Mayeda thinks that "Im Papyrus ist also der
Gedankengang viel glatter," suggesting an earlier tradition
than John v.36–47, wherein he thinks verses 41–44 to be a
Johannine interpolation, obstructing the sequence of thought.

---

[1] Critical opinion, however, is not unanimous in the acceptance of the
Johannine ἐραυνᾶτε as "unambiguous" indicative.

He further illustrates the thesis, by means of the Nicodemus episode (John iii.1–21), that John adapted sources
now lost to us but available to early Christian writers. This
setting is felt to represent a specifically Johannine discourse
rather than a reply to Nicodemus; and much is made of the
shorter form of citation used by Justin (*Apologia* i.61) and
by Pseudo-Justin (*Cohortatio ad gentiles* ix.82) as against
the reading in John iii.5, the presence of "water and Spirit"
marking the point of Johannine insertion. Mayeda thinks
significant, too, Irenaeus' concrete, eschatological use of
"many mansions" (V.xxxvi.2) in contrast to John's obviously spiritual interpretation. He notes further Justin's less
elaborate citation of the Baptist's disclaimer (*Dialogus* 80)
as probably more primitive than the Johannine account
(i.20ff.).

In short, Mayeda feels likewise that Eg. is no mere "mosaic" of excerpts from our canonical Gospels, though the
author may have known some or all of them. And it is "nicht
ausgeschlossen, dass der Verfasser die Quellen nach dem
Gedächtnis wiedergeben hat"; "but it is more likely that he
was freely using and adapting a body of tradition, written
and unwritten." Like Luke and John, the writer of Eg. was
"viel weniger Sammler und mehr Schriftsteller als die Synop-
tiker." Eg. is thus "an example of a genre, of which other
specimens may perhaps turn up hereafter, not represented
in existing remains, part of the popular literature of the early
Church. It is not a 'canonical' Gospel and was written
'wesentlich novellistischer als die Evangelien.' " But "it de-
pends on sources in part independent of the Gospels and
perhaps as old as they, but adds 'keine neuen Materialien
für die Geschichte des Urchristentums, und man lernt keine
neuen Ereignisse des Lebens Jesu kennen.' "

Surely the uniqueness of these fragments among the other
extant remains of early Christian literature may be readily
observed. It is wholesome to note also, in view of the "illiter-

ate" and limited scope of this document, that Mayeda has not attempted with violence to identify Eg. with other surviving "gospels"; nor, on the other hand, does he regard it as another of the "accounts" mentioned by Luke. Certainly among the most interesting of the author's conclusions is his suggestion that the writer of Eg. is probably employing sources involving Synoptic incidents and Johannine sayings representing a tradition both independent of and, in some instances, perhaps prior to, sources used by our evangelists; and that he is consciously employing these sources in a literary effort in which narrative details have been made to replace doctrinal interests, thereby placing Eg. at a point somewhat short of "gospel" status.

In the matter of Johannine sources, of course, there can be no final word; and one must admit the very fascinating possibility that we are here in touch with written or oral materials identical with, or prior to, those used in our Fourth Gospel. It is, however, precarious to argue the fact of such priority or independence from the characteristically mnemonic and elusive citations of Justin (or from those who were possibly dependent upon him). Nor, as we have seen, is it convincing to insist, even in the case of Irenaeus, upon the secondary or divergent character of corresponding canonical items, as compared with some more original source, on the basis of differing patristic contexts and interpretations.

As in the case of the Oxyrhynchus fragments, however, it has been attractive to conjecture by reason of dissimilarities in the rendering of presumably identical canonical details that, here and there, we are possibly in possession of a "lost version" or an "earlier and more original version" than are those recorded in our four Gospels. At no point, however, have these conjectures been sustained. In reference to Eg., for example, it is difficult to resist Professor Cadbury's opinion (*The Peril of Modernizing Jesus*, p. 209 n.) that in Section I we have "another example of the very early editorial introduction of the mission of Jesus. . . Under the influence of the synoptic 'think not that I came,' 'Think not that I will accuse you to the Father' (John v.45) becomes 'Think not that I came to accuse you to my Father.' " Certainly, in view of the, shall we say, "realized eschatology" of the Fourth Evangelist, it seems more convincing to suppose that John was here following, out of whatever necessity, the more "original" source and that Eg. here recorded the more "editorial" version.

In short, the assumption that the writer of Eg. had access to "oral or written" sources prior to or running parallel with those of any one or all four canonical Gospels must remain moot. In at least the one objectively arguable instance of Johannine priority adduced here, the thesis of literary priority or independence cannot be unequivocally claimed for the Egerton composer. One may still question, therefore, whether the conjecture of self-conscious literary licence taken with written or oral sources most satisfactorily explains the readings found in this document. In the course of mnemonic reproduction of canonical sources or tradition, should we not be alert to the unmotivated discrepancies traceable to memory, with both its faulty and compensatingly *creative* facets?

XIV

Summary and Conclusion

From the foregoing discussions it would seem clear that, motivated by the demands of social exigency as well as of faith, Christian writers of the second century deliberately emended the canonical words of Jesus. Hence it is not strange that such "helpful" writings as they produced, being of an essentially didactic and practical character, should evidence variations largely ethical and explanatory in their intent. For in the sober enterprise of fostering a rigorous and active conformity to the will of God, these writers were little concerned with self-conscious literary preoccupations. As a consequence, the stylistic gloss, though present in proportion to individual training and taste, is of relatively limited occurrence. Further, though harmonistic assimilation and juxtaposition of texts bulked large on both the scribal and creatively literary levels, caution must nevertheless be maintained in subsuming under the heading of deliberate harmonization those combinations probably resultant upon merely casual or accidental association of ideas in the course of mnemonic reproduction. It is therefore imperative that there be available a background of consistently accurate citation before significant harmonistic activity can be identified.

That second-century Christianity had varied dogmatic facets is readily evident. Orthodoxy and heresy had equally large stakes in the soteriological import of the things which Jesus did and said; indeed, the gamut of this faith is amply reflected in the literature here dealt with. Yet, with the exception of heterodox activity, dogmatic emendation is, in the main, consistently devoid of radical departures from canonical norms. There is reason to suspect, however, that clearer signs of this interest are quite probably obscured by the very early diligence with which the orthodox and heretics deleted or neutralized one another's efforts in this most vital area of faith.

One is impressed, too, with the more or less definitive scope of inclusion in regard to the traditions and sayings of Jesus evident in the First and Third Gospels. Thus manifold *agrapha*, in some instances independent creations growing out of early Christian experience, are generally not to be thought of as derived from a tradition independent of and running parallel with canonical tradition. They are, in the main, but a series of rearrangements and enlargements of canonical details.

This is so in reference not only to individual sayings but to documents as well; for Jewish-Christian gospels, Papyrus sent, in varying degrees, simply studied or mnemonic adaptations of canonical documents or tradition.

As to canons of accuracy in citation, it is evident that the words of Jesus are not quoted with an appreciably stricter accuracy as a result of authoritative definition of the New Testament canon. The fact that Clement of Alexandria and Tertullian manifest low standards of accuracy in contrast to Irenaeus suggests, too, a personal rather than a universal standard of quotation in reference to dominical utterances. Though Origen, the scholar and textual critic of the third century, quoted extensively and accurately the words of Jesus, clear traces are to be found within his corpus of quotations of deviations from canonical norms for various reasons.

In fine, the words of Jesus were for the early Christians

"Spirit" and they were "life." These words were freely drawn upon and adapted, without literal restraints, in their uniquely authoritative ministry to the "felt needs" of the Christian community.

APPENDIX

A

The Oxyrhynchus Sayings of Jesus [1]

In the following demonstration, the writer has used
H. G. Evelyn White's reconstruction of the Oxyrhynchus
fragments discovered by Messrs. Grenfell and Hunt. These
papyri (1 and 654) are thought to represent but a portion of
a much larger edition of collected utterances of Jesus. In
view of their nature as obvious extracts, many attempts have
been made to discover their origin — their homogeneity having been established, at least with reference to their apparent
lack of tendency, despite their free adaptation of biblical
sources. Yet we must necessarily be modest in our claims of
"homogeneity" regarding what seems to be but a collection
of sayings transmitted without context. Except, too, that the
individual sayings demonsrate no observable tendency, it is
precarious to argue from this the character of a document of
which they are conceivably but a very small part. Thus, in
varying degrees of probability, sameness or similarity of
source, of influence, or even literary dependence presents
each a possible circumstance against which it is difficult to
argue in any attempt to establish a positive setting for our
extracts. Under such conditions, therefore, while positive
association is desirable, it is also hazardous. We shall not,
then, presuppose such a correspondence as Evelyn White
asserts, but shall be here concerned mainly with the treatment given the canonical text wherever this can be detected.

[1] The substance of this essay appeared first as an article in the *Journal
of Biblical Literature*, LXV (1946), 175–183.

Saying I, quoted and discussed above (with differences indicated), Evelyn White believes to have been taken from the *Gospel According to the Hebrews*. Surely one cannot ignore the logic of his arguments. But for the reasons stated, we should hesitate to draw inference as to documentary rapport from such coincidence.

Saying II

λέγει Ἰούδας. τίνες ἄρα οἱ ἕλκοντες ἡμᾶς, καὶ πότε ἐλεύσεται ἡ βασιλεία ἡ ἐν οὐρανοῖς οὖσα; λέγει Ἰησοῦς· τὰ πετεινὰ τοῦ οὐρανοῦ, καὶ τῶν θηρίων ὅτι ὑπὸ τὴν γῆν ἐστιν ἢ ἐπὶ τῆς γῆς, καὶ οἱ ἰχθύες τῆς θαλάσσης, οὗτοι οἱ ἕλκοντες ὑμᾶς· καὶ ἡ βασιλεία τῶν οὐρανῶν ἐντὸς ὑμῶν ἐστι· καὶ ὅστις ἂν ἑαυτὸν γνῷ ταύτην εὑρήσει· καὶ εὑρόντες αὐτὴν ἑαυτοὺς γνώσεσθε ὅτι υἱοὶ καὶ κληρονόμοι ἐστὲ ὑμεῖς τοῦ πατρὸς τοῦ παντοκράτορος, καὶ γνώσεσθε ἑαυτοὺς ἐν θεῷ ὄντας καὶ θεὸν ἐν ὑμῖν. καὶ ὑμεῖς ἐστε ἡ πτόλις θεοῦ.

John xiv.22 has been indicated as the probable source for Judas, the interlocutor. Taylor calls attention also to Matthew vi.26–30, where the fowl of the air and the fish of the sea furnish an object lesson in faith. The idea of the inner residence of the Kingdom may be readily documented from Luke xvii.20. The latter part of the saying, on Evelyn White's observation, seems more like an Alexandrine appendage than a product of Synoptic teaching. Thus, having learned the lesson of faith from the creatures of nature, man becomes conscious of his inner possibilities and personal worth. There is evident, then, a picturesque adaptation of evangelic material with reflective supplement in the interest of the didactic and, perhaps, also of exhortation.

Saying III

λέγει Ἰησοῦς· οὐκ ἀποκνήσει ἄνθρωπος τὴν ὁδὸν εὑρὼν ἐπερωτῆσαι πάντα . . . διαιρῶν περὶ τοῦ τόπου τῆς καθέδρας; εὑρήσετε ὅτι πολλοὶ ἔσονται πρῶτοι ἔσχατοι, καὶ οἱ ἔσχατοι πρῶτοι· καὶ ζωὴν κληρονομήσουσιν.

Evelyn White cites this saying as a typical instance "of that salient characteristic of the Oxyrhynchus collection as a whole — the mixture of elements at once parallel to and divergent from the synoptics." Mark x.31 (Matthew xix.30) is a likely model for the second part of the saying. If, however, the novelty of the first half may not be accounted for "as coming from a lost version of the incident of the Sons of Zebedee," it is a remarkable example of the homiletic expansion of evangelic material consistently observable in this collection.

Saying IV

λέγει Ἰησοῦς· πᾶν τὸ μὴ ἔμπροσθεν τῆς ὄψεώς σου, καὶ τὸ κεκαλυμμένον ἀπό σου ἀποκαλυφθήσεταί σοι· οὐ γάρ ἐστιν κρυπτὸν ὃ οὐ φανερὸν γενήσεται, καὶ τεθαμμένον ὃ οὐκ ἐγερθήσεται.

By means of a brilliant conjecture, Evelyn White, taking note of the present address in the second person singular, connects this passage (through II Clement) with a citation made by Jerome, supposedly from the *Gospel According to the Hebrews*. However this may be, one is immediately attracted here by the free treatment given the Synoptic text by the insertion of these novel details. It has been demonstrated that the present fragment derives partly from the Q tradition and partly from the Lucan version of Mark's tradition (cf. Luke viii.17, xii.2). It will be seen that the bold departures — πᾶν τὸ μὴ ἔμπροσθεν τῆς ὄψεώς σου . . . καὶ τεθαμμένον ὃ οὐκ ἐγερθήσεται — whatever their contexts, are in the nature of a popular and vivid elaboration of their basic details. Hence, whatever the source of these dicta, a homiletic interest, quite probably, will not be found to be inconsistent with the spirit of the document of which they may be a part.

Saying V

ἐξετάζουσιν αὐτὸν οἱ μαθηταὶ αὐτοῦ καὶ λέγουσιν· πῶς νηστεύσομεν,
καὶ πῶς προσευξόμεθα καὶ πῶς ἐλεημοσύνην ποιήσομεν, καὶ τί παρα-
τηρήσομεν τῶν παραδοθέντων; λέγει Ἰησοῦς· οὐκ ἔσεσθε ὡς οἱ ὑποκριταί·
μὴ ποιεῖτε ταῦτα φανερῶς, ἀλλὰ τῆς ἀληθείας ἀντέχεσθε, καὶ ἡ δικαιοσύνη
ὑμῶν ἀποκεκρυμμένη ἔστω· λέγω γάρ· μακάριός ἐστιν ὁ ταῦτα ποιῶν ἐν
κρυπτῷ, ὅτι ἐν φανερῷ ἔσται ὁ μισθὸς αὐτοῦ παρὰ τῷ πατρὶ ὅς ἐστιν ἐν
τοῖς οὐρανοῖς.

Unfortunately, the problems of restoration do not admit
of too confident conclusions regarding the saying in its present form. With necessary reservations, however, the following claims may be made. The restored version reveals at
once a striking correspondence to the Sermon on the Mount
(Matthew vi). In our canonical setting the subjects Alms-
giving, Fasting, and Prayer are discussed by Jesus. The Matthean treatment of the traditions is not met with until chapter xv, though, of course, this need not be the source of the
present mention. As to the character of the saying, one thing
seems clear: We do not seem to have to do with a studied
approximation of evangelic material of the kind expected in
a secondary "gospel." Again, there seems to be no attempt
to reproduce as accurately as memory might allow a set of
Matthean texts. Nor do the verses appear to warrant a
judgment of loose quotation. On the contrary, the sentiments
hang together admirably, it appears, on the view that we
have to do with a sermonic summary and expansion of
familiar material. ἐξετάζουσιν αὐτὸν οἱ μαθηταί serves well as
a homiletic introductory device. The excerpt μὴ ποιεῖτε ταῦτα
φανερῶς . . . μακάριός ἐστιν κτλ is replete with the freedom
accorded uniquely to the homilist.[2] Rather, therefore, than

---

[2] B D and some cursives omit ἐν τῷ φανερῷ from the text of Mt. vi.4 —
a gloss suggested less by way of parallelism, perhaps, than by a religious
conviction "that the blessing for righteousness should be visible to all."

see in this saying possibly "an earlier and more original version of the Sermon on the Mount," as Evelyn White is
tempted to do, this writer is of the opinion that we may account for the observed discrepancies more easily on other
grounds.

Saying VII

λέγει Ἰησοῦς· ἐὰν μὴ νηστεύσητε τὸν κόσμον, οὐ μὴ εὕρητε τὴν
βασιλείαν τοῦ θεοῦ· καὶ ἐὰν μὴ σαββατίσητε τὸ σάββατον, οὐκ ὄψεσθε
τὸν πατέρα.

It seems probable that the present saying might have
grown out of later currents of Christian thought. The sentiment evidences a process of stricter differentiation of a characteristically Christian, as opposed to a Jewish-Christian,
form of thought and of observance. In this extract, the
protases are new, but the sanctions may be found in our
canonical Gospels. Noteworthy in the present connection is
a quotation from Clement of Alexandria (*Stromata* iii.15):
μακάριοι . . . οἱ τοῦ κόσμου νηστεύοντες . . . Justin Martyr (*Dialogus* 12) argues that the "new law" demands
σαββατίζειν διὰ παντός. If, then, νηστεύσητε τὸν κόσνον
means, as is probable, abstention "from evil things"; and if,
on Taylor's suggestion, σαββατίσητε τὸ σάββατον means "to
sanctify the whole week," the intent of the saying is clear.
As Evelyn White shows, the sense of the *logion* is best
paralleled by Matthew v.20. Although the expression "to
find the kingdom of God" is not present in the Synoptics,
it does suggest Matthew vi.33 (Luke xii.31), where "seeking" the Kingdom is enjoined.[3] The Matthean "they shall
see God" (v.8) furnishes a plausible model for the final
clause. Thus there is again evident an attempt, not to quote
our Gospels, but, as we have suggested, to weave freely their

[3] Note A. von Harnack, *Die jüngst entdeckten Sprüche Jesu* (Leipzig,
1897), p. 8.

phrases and spirit into an original fabric, aiming purposely
to embody the authority of their suggestion rather than to
capture the accuracy of their form.

Saying VIII

λέγει Ἰησοῦς· ἔστην ἐν μέσῳ τοῦ κόσμου, καὶ ἐν σαρκὶ ὤφθην αὐτοῖς·
καὶ εὗρον πάντας μεθύοντας, καὶ οὐδένα εὗρον δειψῶντα ἐν αὐτοῖς· καὶ
πονεῖ ἡ ψυχή μου ἐπὶ τοῖς υἱοῖς τῶν ἀνθρώπων, ὅτι τυφλοί εἰσιν τῇ καρδίᾳ
αὐτῶν, καὶ οὐ βλέπουσι τῇ διανοίᾳ αὐτῶν.

Evelyn White presents *Baruch* iii.37 (μετὰ τοῦτο ἐπὶ τῆς
γῆς ὤφθη, καὶ ἐν τοῖς ἀνθρώποις συνανεστράφη) as the passage upon which the introductory sentiment of the saying is
probably dependent. ἐν σαρκί, moreover, may imply pre-
existence and may adumbrate a further Johannine interest,
anti-Docetism — although, as Evelyn White feels, the emphasis here is probably primarily on the humanity of Jesus.
Isaiah xxviii.1 has been adduced as a likely source to account
for μεθύοντας. Synoptic suggestions may be seen also in Luke
xxi.34, xvii.26–27 (Matthew xxiv.38–39), xii.45. δειψῶντα,
in a spiritual sense, which it probably bears here, is to be
found in Matthew v.6. Isaiah lxiii.10 seems a possible Old
Testament parallel with regard to the "grief" of Jesus. Again,
however, ample documentation may be found in our Gospels:
Harnack quotes Matthew xxvi.38; Mark xiv.34; John xii.27.
Further, the Lament over Jerusalem, Matthew xxiii.37 (Luke
xiii.34), seems also suggestive in this connection. The conception of spiritual "blindness" (οἱ τυφλοὶ τῇ καρδίᾳ), Evelyn
White notes, is duplicated in the *Gospel According to
Thomas*, as well as in I Clement (xxxvi). The close approxi-
mation of this sentiment in Matthew xv.14, xxiii.16, and
John ix.39 (quoted by Evelyn White) would seem to point
to its common currency in early Christian tradition.

It will be seen, therefore, that certain characteristic features again emerge in the construction of this saying. What-

ever the source employed, the substance has been, in most
instances, worked up with a distinctive originality. It is not
necessary to deduce any special interest from the specific
adaptations here made. Encratite influence seems gratuitously argued, and preëxistence or anti-Docetism is perhaps
read into our excerpt instead of being implicit in it. Where
evangelic influence is probable, the selection is discursive and
the correspondence one of essence and not of direct expression. Here, as elsewhere in these fragments, the portrayal is a
bold one; the effect dramatic. These are traits which might
fit well, to be sure, into a didactic *cadre*, but better into a
sermon, of which, as we have observed, these features are the
normal rather than the exceptional concomitants.

Saying X

λέγει Ἰησοῦς· ὅπου ἐὰν ὦσιν β', οὐκ εἰσὶν ἄθεοι· καὶ ὅπου εἷς ἐστιν
μόνος, λέγω ἐγώ εἰμι μετ' αὐτοῦ. ἔγειρον τὸν λίθον, κἀκεῖ εὑρήσεις με,
σχίσον τὸ ξύλον, κἀγὼ ἐκεῖ εἰμι.

It has been shown that Matthew xviii.20 is not unlikely
as a source for the first statement of this saying, and that
Matthew xxviii.20 (Evelyn White adds John xvi.32) approximates significantly to the thought of the second. Harnack suggests convincingly Ecclesiastes x.9 as a probable
point of departure for the latter half of the citation. Thus
the tenor is not pantheistic, but the thought is stated in terms
congenial to the normal Christian conviction out of which
it probably arose.

One need not labor the fact of rhetorical licence evident
here at the sacrifice of the form, if not of the substance, of
the sources involved. The phenomenon seems, however, to
vindicate further the suggestion that the material gives evidence of having been employed less by way of formal catechesis (deliberate but doctrinally neutral changes, as we

have noted, being difficult to account for on this basis) than
by way of hortatory address.

Saying XI

λέγει Ἰησοῦς· οὐκ ἔστιν δεκτὸς προφήτης ἐν τῇ πατρίδι αὐτοῦ, οὐδὲ
ἰατρὸς ποιεῖ θεραπείας εἰς τοὺς γεινώσκοντας αὐτόν.

All four Gospels, as Evelyn White observes, furnish a
parallel to the first part of this saying. Matthew xiii.57 and
Mark vi.4 reveal a more direct verbal correspondence to this
clause than does either Luke iv.24 or John iv.44. The employment, however, of the Lucan δεκτός and mention of the
"physician" show influence of the Third Gospel. It is, nevertheless, difficult to suppose that the writer was concerned
with an accurate transcription of our Gospels. On the contrary, Luke iv.23 appears to have been adapted to reinforce
the preceding clause in our saying in a parallelism of thought
and of form. Such independent treatment of evangelic sources
has been a characteristic method of the logographer. Present
variation appears, indeed, harmonious with what has seemed
to be a prior concern for the elaborate and hortatory rather
than for the didactic and direct.

Saying XII

λέγει Ἰησοῦς· πόλις ᾠκοδομημένη ἐπ' ἄκρον ὄρους ὑψηλοῦ καὶ ἐστηριγμένη οὔτε πεσεῖν δύναται οὔτε κρυβῆναι.

A probable dependence of the subject of this saying upon
Matthew v.14 is evident (οὐ δύναται πόλις κρυβῆναι ἐπάνω
ὄρους κειμένη). Evelyn White asserts, quite feasibly, that the
variant ἐπ' ἄκρον τοῦ ὄρους is probably due to the reading of
Isaiah ii.2. Aside, however, from the participle ᾠκοδομημένη,
there is added the apparently superfluous ἐστηριγμένη. The
correspondence of the latter part of our fragment to Matthew
vii.24–25 (Luke vi.47–49) is easily observable. Again, the

added κρυβῆναι indicates a rhetorical interest on the part of the writer.

Saying XIII

λέγει Ἰησοῦς· ἀκούεις εἰς τὸ ἓν ὠτίον σου, τὸ δὲ ἕτερον συνέκλεισας.

This is probably another instance of the kind of picturesque adaptation of canonical material noticeable throughout these sayings. Evelyn White is probably correct in his interpretation that "the logion is, in fact, a masterly analysis of the attitude of those who instinctively close their hearts to unwelcome truth." [4] Matthew xiii.13 and Luke vi.46 perhaps most aptly suggest the limits within which the utterance received form. If, therefore, deductions may be drawn from what appears to have been a more or less consistent literary method, there seems little doubt here as to a purpose concerned primarily with elaborating a set of pregnant sayings of Jesus. In this process the "striking and dramatic" has been studiously cultivated for what may be defensibly termed "sermonic" effect.

[4] Evelyn White, p. 45.

B

Marcion

In reference to Marcion, the fact is impressive that, on documentary considerations, the material to which we now have access does not permit of unambiguous inference regarding his textual activity. It may be seen, for example, that discrepancies recorded by Tertullian are not always clearly to be ascribed to Marcion. For it is now clear that Tertullian's indifferently accurate method of quotation must, in each instance, be soberly taken into account before dogmatic indictment of Marcion, on the basis of alleged textual manipulation, can responsibly be made.

In the following examples we shall be primarily concerned, not with the apprehension of motivation in textual variation, but with an appraisal of such variants in so far as they may be traced to their probable sources. Moreover, we shall not take note of allusions or omissions, since the argument from silence is precariously invoked under such circumstances of transmission. And in the interest of a more or less consecutive demonstration, it has seemed well to follow the order of Harnack's textual reconstruction, as set forth in his *Marcion*, pages 183–240.

Luke vi.35

καὶ ἔσεσθε υἱοὶ θεοῦ.

These words are probably from Marcion's own source. It is thus possible to allege his anti–Old Testament bias to account for the displacement of the canonical ὑψίστου. There is, of course, the Matthean parallel, τοῦ πατρός, indicating, perhaps, opportunity for selection at the source. Since, too, the interest of Tertullian's context centers more about "sonship" than about a particular designation of deity, the possibility of Tertullian's imperfect quotation at this point constitutes an equally probable source for θεοῦ.

Luke vii.28

μείζων πάντων τῶν γεννητῶν γυναικῶν προφήτης Ἰωάννης ἐστίν.

It is quite reasonable, as Harnack thinks, that in the emphasis made of John's greatness with reference to *all* men born of women (an otherwise unattested reading) Marcion implies for John an inferior status over against one not born of woman — Marcion's unborn Christ. It is, however, also possible that the πάντων, if Marcion's, was intended to give greater importance to John and so to enhance, correspondingly, the stature of him whom John preceded in an admittedly subordinate capacity. On the other hand, the emphasis (*omnium*) might well have been Tertullian's own according to the terms of the context, in which Tertullian is himself anxious to stress the unique human status of Christ's forerunner.

Luke viii.21

τίς μοι μήτηρ καὶ τίνες μοι ἀδελφοί, εἰ μὴ οἱ τοὺς λόγους μου ἀκούοντες καὶ ποιοῦντες αὐτούς.

Noticeable is the employment of the Matthean interrogative (twice) in the quotation of this supposedly Lucan verse. Did Marcion hope to achieve emphasis by the "sharpness" of the question? On the other hand, Tertullian's appeal to the incident in the same interrogative form elsewhere [1] gives rise to doubt concerning whose preference is involved. Epi-

---

[1] *De carne Christi* 7.

phanius does not quote the verse but gives this notice: Οὐκ
εἶχεν "ἡ μήτηρ αὐτοῦ καὶ οἱ ἀδελφοὶ αὐτοῦ," ἀλλὰ μόνον "ἡ
μήτηρ σου καὶ οἱ ἀδελφοί σου," [2] calling attention, apparently, to the omission of verse 19 and to the presence of
verse 20 — a somewhat indifferent distinction unless it is
meant to imply an inferior authority attaching to the popular address (σου, verse 20) over against the definite association made by the Evangelist (αὐτοῦ, verse 19). If, then,
the reading may possibly be assigned to Tertullian, it is difficult to urge any special importance of "my words" instead
of the Lucan "God's word." Nor, perhaps significantly, does
Tertullian's refutation turn about this particular variation.

Luke ix.26

ὃς γὰρ ἂν ἐπαισχυνθῇ με κἀγὼ ἐπαισχυνθήσομαι αὐτόν.

Harnack correctly observes that "this verse is not only
abbreviated but also altered." Yet an identical "alteration"
and "abbreviation," apparently Tertullian's own quotation,
occurs in another passage [3] with no obvious implications underlying the change. In fact, in the latter reference one
would not hesitate to call Tertullian's quotation suggestive.
His context demands no more. It would be hazardous, therefore, to attempt to deduce much from the present form of
quotation.

Luke xi.2

πάτερ, ἐλθάτω τὸ ἅγιον πνεῦμά σου ἐφ' ἡμᾶς καὶ καθαρισάτω ἡμᾶς.

This passage (found in Manuscripts B 700 604 162), by
virtue of Tertullian's comment upon the Holy Spirit after his
consideration of πάτερ, Harnack thinks to have stood in
Marcion's New Testament text. And despite the reconstruc-

---

[2] Epiph., *Schol.* 12.
[3] *De carne Christi* 5.

tion on the basis of allusion, the reading is intrinsically noteworthy.

Rendel Harris thinks the sentiment to represent a Montanist gloss corresponding to other and similar features observed in the Western text of Luke and the Acts.[4] Professor Cadbury, on the contrary, believes that such references to the Holy Spirit are wholly in keeping with Luke's own interests. He states: "For Luke the petition 'May thy holy Spirit come upon us and cleanse us,' would be a reasonable equivalent for 'May thy kingdom come'; and there is some textual evidence that the former rather than the latter was actually written by him in the Lord's Prayer."[5] Indeed, the homogeneous character of Luke-Acts with regard to both interest and style, according to Professor Cadbury's demonstration, renders improbable the necessity of appeal to an extraneous source to account for the present reading.[6]

Luke x.21

Εὐχαριστῶ σοι καὶ ἐξομολογοῦμαι, κύριε τοῦ οὐρανοῦ, ὅτι ἄτινα ἦν κρυπτὰ σοφοῖς καὶ συνετοῖς ἀπεκάλυψας νηπίοις.

Certainly it is possible to contend that tendentious alterations are to be seen in ἄτινα ἦν κρυπτά for ἀπέκρυψας and in the omission of τῆς γῆς. On the other hand, Tertullian's argument seems purposefully to suggest the setting forth of the idea of concealment in a kind of neutral tableau in order the more impressively to identify the "hiding" with Marcion's God. Further, the Lord of Heaven, Tertullian con-

---

[4] *A Study of Codex Bezae* (Cambridge, England, 1891), pp. 26f.

[5] *The Making of Luke-Acts* (New York, 1927), pp. 269ff.; 286ff.

[6] Canon Streeter (*The Four Gospels*, pp. 276–278) is convinced, on textual grounds, that the above reading "stood in the text of Marcion, and from Tertullian's comment on this it is not at all clear that his own text was in this respect different from Marcion's." He further assigns this reading, along with other matter in Lk. xi.1–4, to what he considers Luke's peculiar source, L.

tinues, by reason of this identification, is inevitably Marcion's God, the Father of Christ. Is it not also possible, therefore, that the new arrangement may be but a concession to the logical necessities of Tertullian's arguments?

Luke xi.42

τὴν κλῆσιν for τὴν κρίσιν.

On the authority of both Tertullian and Epiphanius it is reasonably probable that here we are in possession of a Marcionite reading. On the basis of alleged Marcionite premises in reference to the antithetical contrasts obtaining between the Creator and the God of Love, one may see the obvious compatibility of this reading with these principles.

Luke xiii.28

ὅτε πάντας τοὺς δικαίους εἰσερχομένους ἴδητε ἐν τῇ βασιλείᾳ τοῦ θεοῦ, ὑμᾶς δὲ κρατουμένους ἔξω.

This reading receives the common support of Tertullian and Epiphanius. It is quite possible that there is reflected in the omission of the Patriarchs (and the substitution of "the righteous") an expression of Marcion's reputed anti-Jewish sentiment — although the recognition of Moses and the prophets elsewhere (xii.29) is also to be noted. The reading κρατουμένους for ἐκβαλλομένους may possibly adumbrate a doctrinal bias, on Marcion's supposed principles, in favor of the good God by thus concealing any suggestion of judgment at his hand.

Luke xvi.17

εὐκοπώτερον δέ ἐστιν τὸν οὐρανὸν καὶ τὴν γῆν παρελθεῖν ἢ τῶν λόγων μου μίαν κεραίαν πεσεῖν.[7]

---

[7] Canonical evidence also (Lk. xxi.33 and parallels) may be advanced to account for the reading "my words" without the inclusion of "the law."

The passage so recorded perhaps justifies Harnack's judgment of the existence of a "tendentious emendation." But
the passage from Tertullian (iv.33) on which the reconstruction is based reads: "transeat igitur caelum et terra
citius, sicut et lex et prophetae, quam unus apex verborum
domini." Tertullian follows with the comment: "verbum
enim, inquit Esaias, dei nostri manet in aevum." It seems
apparent, therefore, that Tertullian is merely buttressing his
contention (the divine authority of John's utterances with
reference to the Kingdom of God) by means of biblical appeal in proof of the supremacy of God's word. The "tendency," therefore, along with the reading, is with difficulty
attributed to Marcion.

Luke xxii.70

οὐ οὖν ὁ υἱὸς τοῦ θεοῦ εἶ; ὁ δὲ ἀπεκρίθη· ὑμεῖς λέγετε.

Tertullian comments upon the omission of ὅτι ἐγώ εἰμι:
"quasi 'non ego.' " Harnack speaks here also of a "cancella-
tion," on the ground that an admission, that is, the canonical
Lucan reading at this point, would have been fatal to Marcion's principles. It is indeed probable that we have here an
omission, and possibly a deliberate one. It is not, however,
immediately clear how meaning and motive can be reasonably deduced from *vos dicitis* without placing a corresponding construction upon Σὺ λέγεις (Mark xv.2 and parallel),
unless it be granted that such reasoning apropos of the
Marcionite reading is based on assumptions that are at once
a priori and arbitrary.

Luke xxiv.39

ἴδετε τὰς χεῖράς μου καὶ τοὺς πόδας μου, ὅτι ἐγώ εἰμι αὐτός, ὅτι πνεῦμα
ὀστέα οὐκ ἔχει, καθὼς ἐμὲ θεωρεῖτε ἔχοντα.

Marcion was supposedly hostile to the idea of a bodily resurrection. Tertullian is therefore at a loss to account for his inclusion of this verse, unless, he conjectures, it is to lend credence to his former omissions. To be sure, the ψηλαφήσατε κτλ are lacking. The omission of σάρκα is perhaps also noteworthy. Yet Jesus' denial of his existence in a phantasmal state (or, in fact, the very fact of the inclusion of the incident at all) militates, it would seem, against categorical dogmatic inference.

C

Codex Bezae

In considering briefly some of the so-called Western readings found in Codex D, we shall be concerned primarily with observing the transmission of gospel material which has been subject to a textual history and to a set of theological and practical interests different from those attaching to corresponding passages in our canonical Gospels. With significance for the whole body of citations discussed in this work, F. C. Grant states of this transmission: "As for the process by which the tradition was handed down, the analysis of material shows that the gospel narratives, anecdotes, parables, and sayings were told, not in order to provide biographical data for a literary- and historically-minded later generation, but in order to answer the felt needs of the early Christians themselves." [1] The readings to be recorded, then, are not presented as primary sources for the sayings of Jesus. But, issuing from sources oral and written, they do present instructive instances of the early impress of orthodox interests upon evangelic tradition with regard to the words of Jesus.

Westcott and Hort adjudge "love of paraphrase" to be the hallmark of Western readings. This, along with a fondness for details — picturesque, explanatory, dogmatic,[2] and

[1] "Form Criticism: A New Method of Research," *Religion in Life*, III (1934), 360.

[2] Syr^s B W Θ support D in the omission of Lk. xxiii.34. Although Rendel Harris thinks its omission to have been "provoked by the anti-Judaic polemic, arising very early in the history of the Church," there is also the

sometimes, perhaps, technical — may be seen in the following examples.

Luke xvi.23

ὁρᾷ ᾿Αβραὰμ ἀπὸ μακρόθεν καὶ Λάζαρον ἐν τῷ κόλπῳ αὐτοῦ ἀναπαυόμενον.

Matthew xxv.1

ἐξῆλθον εἰς ἀπάντησιν τοῦ νυμφίου καὶ τῆς νύμφης.[3]

Luke xix.44

καὶ οὐκ ἀφήσουσιν λίθον ἐπὶ λίθον ἐν ὅλῃ σοι.

Matthew x.23

ὅταν δὲ διώκωσιν ὑμᾶς ἐν τῇ πόλει ταύτῃ φεύγετε εἰς τὴν ἄλλην· ἐὰν δὲ ἐν τῇ ἄλλῃ διώκωσιν ὑμᾶς, φεύγετε εἰς τὴν ἄλλην.

Luke v.10 [4]

ὁ δὲ εἶπεν αὐτοῖς, Δεῦτε καὶ μὴ γίνεσθε ἁλιεῖς ἰχθύων, ποιήσω γὰρ ὑμᾶς ἁλιεῖς ἀνθρώπων.

Luke x.16

ὁ ἀκούων ὑμῶν ἐμοῦ ἀκούει, καὶ ὁ ἀθετῶν ὑμᾶς ἐμὲ ἀθετεῖ· ὁ δὲ ἐμοῦ ἀκούων ἀκούει τοῦ ἀποστείλαντός με.

---

equally valid possibility that these words have been inserted into the original text of Luke. In Mt. vi.10 a clearer example of omission in Codex D is afforded by the absence of the comparative adverb ὡς (see discussion in Additional Note on Dogmatic Motivation, p. 68).

[3] Of this reading F. C. Burkitt asserts (*The Journal of Theological Studies*, XXX [1929], 270): "The bride, whether explicitly mentioned or not, must be thought of as with the bridegroom. . . I suggest that the longer text is the true text, and that the various reading (i.e. the omission of 'and the bride') was caused by an early reviser who had less interest in the consistency of the picture than in the Christian conception of the expected second coming of the Lord Jesus to claim His Bride the Church. The conception of the Church as the Bride of Christ . . . remains a metaphor which can be followed out or dropped; it is not always inevitable, and I am quite sure it is not the metaphor implied in the Parable of the Ten Virgins."

[4] Cf. Mk. i.17 (Mt. iv.19).

Matthew xxv.41

τὸ πῦρ τὸ αἰώνιον, ὃ ἡτοίμασεν ὁ πατήρ μου τῷ διαβόλῳ καὶ τοῖς ἀγγέλοις αὐτοῦ.

Luke xiii.8

σκάψω περὶ αὐτὴν καὶ βάλω κόφινον κοπρίων.

Luke ix.55

στραφεὶς δὲ ἐπετίμησεν αὐτοῖς καὶ εἶπεν· οὐκ οἴδατε ποίου πνεύματός ἐστε;

Matthew v.22

πᾶς ὁ ὀργιζόμενος τῷ ἀδελφῷ αὐτοῦ εἰκῆ, ἔνοχος ἔσται τῇ κρίσει.

It has been urged that this is the original reading for the passage here cited. Certainly much early authority may be adduced in its favor. Yet there is Mark iii.5 to be "explained away" on this view, although the reading might have arisen independently of any such apologetic interest. In any case, the motive of ethical accommodation most reasonably accounts for the present insertion.

Luke vi.5

τῇ αὐτῇ ἡμέρᾳ θεασάμενός τινα ἐργαζόμενον τῷ σαββάτῳ εἶπεν αὐτῷ· ἄνθρωπε, εἰ μὲν οἶδας τί ποιεῖς, μακάριος εἶ· εἰ δὲ μὴ οἶδας, ἐπικατάρατος καὶ παραβάτης εἶ τοῦ νόμου.

The origin of this saying is unknown. Montefiore condemns it as ungenuine on the assumption that Jesus would scarcely have "gone so far in open approval of a direct violation of one of the most fundamental injunctions of the Law." We should venture the suggestion, however, that the purport of the saying is not in defense of Sabbath-breaking. The saving "knowledge," it may be noted, is highly conditional and vague; the alternative judgment, on the other hand, is harsh and decisive. The established institution of

the Law is importantly at stake. Less, then, from the statement than from its dominant suggestion it would seem possible to argue a probable legal tendency in this "subtle,"
reflective assertion.

Matthew xx.28; cf. Luke xiv.8–10

ὑμεῖς δὲ ζητεῖτε ἐκ μικροῦ αὐξῆσαι καὶ ἐκ μείζονος ἔλαττόν εἶναι·
εἰσερχόμενοι δὲ καὶ παρακληθέντες δειπνῆσαι, μὴ ἀνακλίνεσθε εἰς τοὺς
ἐξέχοντας τόπους, μήποτε ἐνδοξότερός σου ἐπέλθῃ, καὶ προσελθὼν ὁ
δειπνοκλήτωρ εἴπῃ σοι· ἔτι κάτω χώρει, καὶ καταισχυνθήσῃ· ἐὰν δὲ ἀνα-
πέσῃς εἰς τὸν ἥττονα τόπον καὶ ἐπέλθῃ ἥττων, ἐρεῖ σοι ὁ δειπνοκλήτωρ·
σύναγε ἔτι ἄνω, καὶ ἔσται σοι τοῦτο χρήσιμον.

There does not seem to be a sufficiently close relation between the two parts of this verse to necessitate one's assum-
ing their circulation as an original unit. It is perhaps significant, too, that they receive separate authentication in
Leo and Hilary, respectively. The latter sentiment may
well be an oral counterpart to Luke xiv.8–10. Differences
could possibly be reconciled on this assumption. The shorter
dictum, on the other hand, demonstrates a kind of elaboration
observable in previous examples of paraphrastic activity,
though perhaps so worded in its source, "written or oral."

Matthew xvi.2–3

ὀψίας γενομένης λέγετε· εὐδία, πυρράζει γὰρ ὁ οὐρανός· καὶ πρωΐ·
σήμερον χειμών, πυρράζει γὰρ στυγνάζων ὁ οὐρανός. τὸ μὲν πρόσωπον
τοῦ οὐρανοῦ γινώσκετε διακρίνειν, τὰ δὲ σημεῖα τῶν καιρῶν οὐ δύνασθε;

This saying relative to the discerning of the "signs of the
time" has been rejected with reasonable certainty, on textual grounds, from the text of Matthew at this point. The
sentiment suggests immediately a similar saying in Luke
(xii.54ff.). Although, as Dr. Hatch thinks,[5] the sayings
are "sufficiently unlike" to make improbable a common

---

[5] *The Western Text of the Gospels* (Evanston, Ill., 1937), p. 18.

source, they do represent, in all probability, a not uncommon effort to conceptualize apocalyptic through the medium of natural imagery.

John vii.53–viii.11

For our purpose we need not attempt to discuss the critical probabilities attaching to the *Pericope Adulterae*. Suffice it to say that it is thought to be a comparatively late Western insertion belonging originally to "an extraneous, independent source." Neither Origen nor Tertullian refers to this incident in his discussions of the Fourth Gospel where such mention might be revelant. The story is assuredly excluded from the New Testament on textual grounds. And, despite its self-vindicating features, its ascription to Jesus must be made on purely subjective considerations. The reference in the *Apostolic Constitutions* to this *pericope* as an authority for the reception of penitents is illustrative of a practical interest in the Christian community making for its survival quite apart from its own intrinsically compelling appeal.

The changes thus noted in Codex D exemplify the history of the New Testament text as a living entity in widespread areas of the Christian community. Additions were made, omissions effected, and various editorial devices often applied.[6] Oral tradition is quite probably a source for some of the variants noted. Perhaps private interpolation is also here to be seen. In any case, variation has been not only suffered but also scrupulously preserved in response "to the felt needs of the early Christians themselves." [7]

---

[6] The insertion of διὸ λέγω ὑμῖν (Lk. xvi.8), making, apparently, for smoothness, and the prefacing of the Lord's Prayer (Lk. xi.2) with the sentiment of Mt. vi.7, making for "characteristic fullness," are also noteworthy.

[7] A fresh, scholarly survey of the history of scientific investigations into the character of Codex Bezae is that by A. F. J. Klijn, *A Survey of the Researches into the Western Texts of the Gospels and Acts* (Utrecht, 1949).

D

Origen

The task to which we shall give attention in reference to Origen is a modest one; the subsequent findings, therefore, are more properly a supplement to than a chapter in the development of this monograph. We are not concerned here with the problem of motivation underlying variant renderings of the text. Because of Origen's especially keen interest for readings and texts, however, and because of the relatively more mature status of the New Testament canon in the third century than in the second, it has seemed well to inquire into the treatment of the text of the New Testament given by one of his intellectual stature and fervent convictions. Under certain general headings we shall therefore record, not discuss, such variants as have here been collected. Further, in the interest of a more accurate representation of Origen's method of citation, we shall not take account of the Latin renderings of his works. Again, of course, the words of Jesus determine the limits of this inquiry.

I. LOOSE OR MNEMONIC QUOTATION

Excerpta in Psalmos col. 132D (Matthew xxv.37, 40) * [1]

ὥσπερ λέγει· Τοῦτον ἔθρεψας, ἐμὲ ἔθρεψας·

[1] Starred (*) readings are those selected from Migne's *Patrologia Graeca*. Renderings from this source, of course, must always be accepted guardedly. In these instances textual information is not yet available in *Die Griechischen Christlichen Schriftsteller* series, from which the remaining quotations of Origen are derived.

Selecta in Psalmos col. 1264A (Luke xxii.29) *

Κἀγὼ θήσομαι ὑμῖν Διαθήκην, ἐσθίειν καὶ πίνειν ἐπὶ τῆς τραπέζης τοῦ πατρὸς ἐν τῇ ἀληθείᾳ.

Homilia in Jeremiam iv.3 (Matthew xxiv.24; cf. II Thess. ii. 3–4)

ἐν τῷ εὐαγγελίῳ ὑπὸ τοῦ σωτῆρος εἰρημένων . . . ποιήσει σημεῖα καὶ τέρατα ὁ ἐλευσόμενος.

Commentarius in Joannem x.20 (Luke xix.43–44)

ὅτι ἥξουσιν ἡμέραι ἐπὶ σὲ καὶ περικυκλώσουσιν καὶ συνέξουσί σε πάντοθεν, καὶ ἐδαφιοῦσί σε καὶ τὰ τέκνα σου . . .

Commentarius in Joannem xix.20 (John xv.19)

φησὶ γοῦν τοῖς μαθηταῖς· Ἐκ τοῦ κόσμου ἦτε, κἀγὼ ἐξελεξάμην ὑμᾶς ἐκ τοῦ κόσμου, καὶ οὐκέτι ἐστὲ ἐκ τοῦ κόσμου.

Commentarius in Joannem i.11 (Matthew xxv.40)

φησὶ τοῖς πεποιηκόσι· Τούτοις ὃ ἐποιήσατε ἐμοὶ ἐποιήσατε.

De Principiis iv.1 (Matthew vii.22; cf. Luke xiii. 26–27) [2]

πολλοὶ ἐροῦσί μοι ἐν ἐκείνῃ τῇ ἡμέρᾳ· κύριε, κύριε, οὐ τῷ ὀνόματί σου ἐφάγομεν καὶ τῷ ὀνόματί σου ἐπίομεν καὶ τῷ ὀνόματί σου δαιμόνια ἐξεβάλομεν; καὶ ἐρῶ αὐτοῖς κτλ.

Contra Celsum viii.74 (cf. Luke xix.17, xvi.10)

πρὸς οὓς λέγοιτο ἄν· ἐν ἐλαχίστῃ πόλει πιστὸς ἐγένου, ἧκε καὶ ἐπὶ τὴν μεγάλην.

Contra Celsum iii.32 (Matthew xxvii.46)

πάτερ, ἱνατί με ἐγκατέλιπες;

Scholia in Matthaeum col. 239A (Luke xii.32) *

Διὸ καὶ ἔλεγε· Μὴ φοβοῦ, μικρὸν ποίμνιον ὅτι εὐδόκησεν ὁ θεὸς ἐν σοί.

---

[2] Perhaps rather an instance of conflation.

2. CONFLATION [3]

Expositio in Proverbia col. 209A (Matthew xvi.26; Luke ix.25) *

Τί ὠφεληθήσεται ἄνθρωπος ἐὰν τὸν κόσμον ὅλον κερδήσῃ, τὴν δὲ ψυχὴν αὐτοῦ ἀπολέσῃ καὶ ζημιωθῇ; [4]

Commentarius in Matthaeum xii.32 (Matthew xvi.28, 27) [5]

τί δηλοῦται ἐν τῷ ἰδεῖν τὸν υἱὸν τοῦ ἀνθρώπου ἐρχόμενον ἐν τῇ βασιλείᾳ αὐτοῦ καὶ ἐν τῇ δόξῃ αὐτοῦ . . .

Homilia in Jeremiam xii.2 (Matthew xxvi.28; Luke xxii.20)

λέγει αὐτοῖς· λάβετε, πίετε, τοῦτό ·μού ἐστι τὸ αἷμα τὸ ὑπὲρ ὑμῶν ἐκχυ- νόμενον εἰς ἄφεσιν ἁμαρτιῶν.

Homilia in Jeremiam xix.13 (Mark xiv.15; Luke xi.25)

εἶπε . . . ἐκεῖνος ὑμῖν δείξει ἀνάγαιον μέγα, ἐστρωμένον, σεσαρωμένον, ἕτοιμον . . .

Commentarius in Joannem xxxii.32 (Matthew x.38; Luke xiv.27)

Ὃς ἂν μὴ ἄρῃ τὸν σταυρὸν αὐτοῦ καὶ ἀκολουθήσει ὀπίσω μου, οὐκ ἔστιν μου ἄξιος εἶναι μαθητής.

Commentarius in Joannem xx.2 (Luke xii.42; cf. Matthew xxiv.49)

Τίς ἄρα ἐστὶν ὁ πιστὸς καὶ φρόνιμος οἰκονόμος, ὃν καταστήσει ὁ κύριος ἐπὶ τῆς οἰκετίας αὐτοῦ, τοῦ διδόναι ἐν καιρῷ τὸ σιτομέτριον τοῖς συνδούλοις ἑαυτοῦ;

Commentarius in Joannem i.11 (Matthew xxvi.13; cf. Matthew xxiv.14)

γέγραπται· Ὅπου ἂν κηρυχθῇ τὸ εὐαγγέλιον τοῦτο ἐν πᾶσι τοῖς ἔθνεσι, λαληθήσεται καὶ ὃ ἐποίησεν αὕτη εἰς μνημόσυνον αὐτῆς.

[3] Variants recorded under this heading may be regarded also as quota- tions made from memory.
[4] A similar reading is recorded in *Comm. in Joan.* xix.15.
[5] Note also xii.31.

Commentarius in Joannem i.29 (John xv.15; Luke xxii.28)

Οὐκέτι ὑμᾶς λέγω δούλους, ὅτι ὁ δοῦλος οὐκ οἶδε τί τὸ θέλημα τοῦ κυρίου αὐτοῦ· ἀλλὰ λέγω ὑμᾶς φίλους, ὅτι διαμεμενήκατε μετ' ἐμοῦ ἐν πᾶσι τοῖς πειρασμοῖς μου.

Contra Celsum xiii.18 (Cf. Matthew vii.24 and parallels)

ἐάν τις ἀκούῃ μου τοὺς λόγους καὶ ποιῇ αὐτούς, ἐγὼ καὶ ὁ πατήρ μου ἐλευσόμεθα πρὸς αὐτὸν καὶ μονὴν παρ' αὐτῷ ποιησόμεθα.

3. IMPROVEMENT AND INTERPRETATION [6]

Expositio in Proverbia col. 236A (John viii.31) *

ὁ Σωτήρ . . . φησίν· Ἐὰν ὑμεῖς μείνητε ἐν τῷ λόγῳ τῷ ἐμῷ, ἀληθῶς μαθηταί μου ἐστέ· καὶ ἡ ἀλήθεια ἠλευθέρωσεν ἐκ τῆς κατάρας τοῦ νόμου.

Libellus de Oratione col. 508A (John vi.32) *

Μωϋσῆς δέδωκεν ὑμῖν τὸν ἄρτον ἐκ τοῦ οὐρανοῦ, οὐ τὸν ἀληθινόν, ἀλλ' ὁ πατήρ μου δίδωσιν ὑμῖν τὸν ἄρτον ἐκ τοῦ οὐρανοῦ τὸν ἀληθινόν.

Libellus de Oratione col. 448B (Cf. Luke xi.13) *

καὶ δίδωσιν ὁ πατὴρ τὸ ἀγαθὸν δόμα ὧν ἐξ οὐρανοῦ τοῖς αἰτοῦσιν αὐτον.

Homilia in Jeremiam xiv.5 (Cf. Luke xi.49, vii.35)

καὶ ἐν τῷ εὐαγγελίῳ ἀναγέγραπται· καὶ ἀποστέλλει ἡ σοφία τὰ τέκνα αὐτῆς.

Commentarius in Matthaeum xvii.34 (Luke xx.34)

κατὰ μὲν τὸν Λουκᾶν . . . οἱ υἱοὶ τοῦ αἰῶνος τούτου γεννῶσι καὶ γεννῶν-ται, γαμοῦσι καὶ γαμίσκονται.

Homilia in Jeremiam i.13 (Matthew v.11–12)

μακάριοί ἐστε ὅταν ὀνειδίζωσιν ὑμᾶς καὶ διώκωσι καὶ εἴπωσι πᾶν πονηρὸν ῥῆμα καθ' ὑμῶν ψευδόμενοι ἕνεκεν ἐμοῦ.

[6] See p. 78 for a probable instance of explanatory variation traceable to Origen.

Commentarius in Joannem xxxii.11 (Matthew vii.23)

Ἀποχωρεῖτε ἀπ' ἐμοῦ· οὐδέποτε ἔγνων ὑμᾶς, ὅτι ἐργάται ἐστὲ ἀδικίας.

Commentarius in Joannem xxxii.13 (Luke vi.40)

ἐν δὲ τῷ κατὰ Λουκᾶν . . . κατηρτισμένος δὲ πᾶς ἔστω ὡς ὁ διδάσκαλος αὐτοῦ.

Commentarius in Joannem xxxii.7 (Matthew xxv.29)

παντὶ τῷ ἔχοντι δοθήσεται καὶ προστεθήσεται.

Contra Celsum viii.14 (John xiv.27)

οὐ καθὼς ὁ κόσμος δίδωσιν εἰρήνην, κἀγὼ δίδωμι ὑμῖν εἰρήνην.

4. SPECIAL INTEREST

Commentarius in Joannem xiii.37 (John xiv.28) [7]

ὁ πατὴρ ὁ πέμψας με μείζων μού ἐστιν.

Selecta in Psalmos col. 1569A (John xvi.32) *

Οὐκ εἰμὶ μόνος, ἀλλ' ἐγὼ καὶ ὁ πέμψας με πατήρ.

Selecta in Psalmos col. 1268B (Matthew xviii.10) *

Μὴ καταφρονήσητε γάρ, θησὶν ὁ Σωτήρ, ἑνὸς τούτων τῶν μικρῶν τῶν ἐν τῇ Ἐκκλησίᾳ·

Contra Celsum v.11 (Luke xviii.19)

οὐδεὶς ἀγαθὸς εἰ μὴ εἷς, ὁ θεὸς ὁ πατήρ.[8]

[7] An interesting commentary upon some of the emphases here noted is presented in the following statement (*Comm. in Joan.* vi.39): ὁ γὰρ πέμψας αὐτὸν πατήρ . . . οὗτος καὶ μόνος ἀγαθὸς καὶ μείζων τοῦ πεμφθέντος.

[8] For scientific methodology in an adequate study of the citations of Origen, a work of fundamental importance, among others, would be E. Hautsch's *Die Evangelienzitate des Origines*, *TU*, XXXIV, 2 (Leipzig, 1909).

Reference Index

General Index

HARVARD HISTORICAL MONOGRAPHS